How Wars End

JAN VAN AKEN

How Wars End

A hopeful history
of making peace

Translated by Jo Heinrich

ITHAKA

First published in the UK in 2025 by Ithaka Press
An imprint of Bonnier Books UK
5th Floor, HYLO, 103–105 Bunhill Row,
London, EC1Y 8LZ

Owned by Bonnier Books
Sveavägen 56, Stockholm, Sweden

Hardback – 978-1-80418-965-8
Trade Paperback – 978-1-7851-2432-7
Ebook – 978-1-80418-966-5
Audiobook – 978-1-80418-967-2

All rights reserved. No part of the publication may be reproduced, stored in a retrieval system, transmitted or circulated in any form or by any means, electronic, mechanical, photocopying, recording or otherwise, without prior permission in writing of the publisher.

A CIP catalogue of this book is available from the British Library.

Typeset by IDSUK (Data Connection) Ltd
Printed and bound by Clays Ltd, Elcograf S.p.A.

1 3 5 7 9 10 8 6 4 2

Copyright © by Ullstein Buchverlage GmbH Berlin. Published in 2024 by Econ Verlag
Translation copyright © by Jo Heinrich 2025

Jan Van Aken and Jo Heinrich have asserted their moral right to be identified as the author and translator of this Work in accordance with the Copyright, Designs and Patents Act 1988.

Every reasonable effort has been made to trace copyright holders of material reproduced in this book, but if any have been inadvertently overlooked the publishers would be glad to hear from them.

www.bonnierbooks.co.uk

Contents

Introduction — 1

Making peace

1. What does it take to start peace negotiations? — 7
2. Peace negotiations — 19
3. Closing the wounds: justice for the victims — 39
4. Local conflict management — 54
5. UN peacekeeping forces: when trust hits rock bottom — 65
6. Weapons inspections — 82
7. Using science against war propaganda — 97
8. News makes war — 110
9. Arms exports out of control — 123
10. Supplying arms or prioritising a civil approach? — 138
11. Sanctions and their side effects — 145
12. War starts here. Peace too — 160
13. Disarmament from above and from below — 173

But now, down to specifics: What about Ukraine and the Middle East?

14. Peace for Ukraine? — 189
15. Peace needs vision: Israel and Palestine — 201

Epilogue: Dispelling tanks from our thoughts — 212
Acknowledgements — 217
Notes — 219

INTRODUCTION

*Negotiations are the continuation of war
in a different theater of operations*[1]

Many truths we believed to be certain have been lost in recent years. Ensuring peace is made and maintained *without weapons* – wasn't that always the right thing to do? But since 2022, many people have been asking themselves, 'Shouldn't Ukraine be allowed to defend itself against Russia's brutal attack? How can it achieve peace without weapons and without self-defence? How else can it prevent Russia taking over the entire country?' The same applies to the Middle East; here, too, a future without weapons seems hard to imagine.

This book is not a detailed master plan for ending the conflict in the Middle East or the Russian war of aggression in Ukraine: that simply doesn't exist. But there are experiences we can learn from that will help us deal with current wars and lead to a more peaceful tomorrow. This book will demonstrate how weapons might eventually be laid aside, even in the most complicated situations and bloodiest conflicts, and how paths have been cleared to make lasting peace.

There are so many inspiring examples in history, so much courage and hope that can be taken from the peaceful settlement of various conflicts, that I'm profoundly convinced there can (almost) always be amicable paths to peace. They are often not easy, and they might come at a price – but it's a price that means less death, suffering and destruction. Three-quarters of all armed conflicts in recent decades have ended in a peace agreement.²

Examples from all over the world can show us how peace talks work and what it takes for them to even begin. What role can a European country, for example, play in supporting peace processes in other parts of the world? What can be done to prevent conflicts escalating in the first place and to stop wars before they've even started? This book will look back into history, at the successes and failures of various peace processes over the years, and look forward, to the many paths available to more peaceful resolution of conflict.

I have interwoven the latest findings in peace research with stories from real life, as well as from my personal experience. I've been working with issues relating to disarmament and peace for 25 years now, which is a little unusual for someone who trained as a biologist. Here's how it came about. Ever since I started my studies, I've been concerned with the risks of genetic engineering, in all its variations. I did some research into this subject at university and organised Greenpeace campaigns. During that time, the question of whether genetic engineering might be relevant to war came up again and again, because it could make biological warfare even more dangerous. It was a question that practically never came up in public discussion. I kept ignoring it too, until I came across the book *The Cobra Event* by Richard Preston in 1999, in which a genetically modified supervirus threatens humanity. It was exaggerated and over the top, but fast-paced, and I found it an entertaining read. A few months later, an American colleague and I were inspired by it and came up with the idea of taking a closer look at this kind of risk together. In a little restaurant in New York City, we developed the concept of a small non-governmental organisation (NGO), the Sunshine Project, which over the next few years researched a few scandals relating to genetic engineering and biological weapons.

Introduction

I was already involved in disarmament issues; since then, I've been doing many different forms of work in this area, and I've encountered a huge range of ways and means to achieve peaceful conflict resolution. As a biological weapons inspector for the United Nations, I was able to experience first-hand what peaceful alternatives there could have been to military violence in Iraq in 2003, as well as how political and economic interests sometimes deliberately block a more peaceful path to conflict resolution. During my time at Greenpeace International, I worked on nuclear disarmament initiatives in the Middle East, and as a member of the German parliament I was able to gain a first-hand understanding of the situations – and potential solutions – in various conflict regions. Whether it was local initiatives for civilian crisis prevention in South Sudan, the International Atomic Energy Agency's investigations into Iran's nuclear programme, German arms being supplied to war zones, or a parliamentary committee of inquiry looking into the Kunduz bombing in Afghanistan, everywhere I went I came across peaceful alternatives and civil opportunities for resolving conflict, which unfortunately all too often failed due to the selfish interests of individual stakeholders.

This book will use examples to trace how wars have come to an end, how new flare-ups of violence were prevented, and how lasting peace was able to be reached – and it will also look at our role in many of the world's conflicts. After all, whether and how rich countries become involved all too often depends on what benefits them and their economies. When we're ensuring that raw materials stay cheap and access to fossil fuels remains secure, human rights and peace often fall by the wayside, and one nation invading a neighbour is quickly excused. If we want to block refugee routes long before they can reach the Mediterranean, we might make even the worst offenders into our 'partners'. If we can forge dirty deals by supplying arms, we shouldn't be surprised if the weapons are actually used. While the whole world knew that Assad's regime in Syria was producing vast quantities of the chemical weapon sarin, European companies still carried on supplying the raw chemicals to Syria – possibly because the Syrian secret service was considered indispensable in the 'war on terror'.

This cynicism – some might call it realpolitik – is a huge contrast to the everyday heroes who work tirelessly in their communities, their countries and their continents to ensure peace or to restore it: the people who resolve conflicts by civil means, who mediate in wars, who reconcile and commemorate, who fight injustices, who take action against impunity or who take great risks to oppose the illusory solution of armed violence. This is also a book about them, and for them. Long may they inspire us to make our own contribution to a peaceful, just world.

Making Peace

1

WHAT DOES IT TAKE TO START PEACE NEGOTIATIONS?

The Syrian civil war could have come to an end as early as 2012. Unfortunately, though, in war it's not usually the stronger side that gives in, and it's only too seldom that anyone wants to be the bigger person.

In early 2011, the Arab Spring had arrived in Syria, with widespread demonstrations against Bashar al-Assad's regime. When the police opened fire on peaceful demonstrators that March, many people were killed. Violence escalated very quickly, and Syria found itself in the midst of a bloody civil war. Tens of thousands of soldiers deserted and formed the Free Syrian Army. Western nations – and many others – supported the rebels, and Bashar al-Assad came under increasing pressure. In 2012, it looked as if he scarcely stood a chance in military terms.

Faced with this situation, Assad proposed a peaceful transfer of power: he offered to step down in 2014, clearing the way for a new government.[3] To this day, we'll never know how serious he was, or what loopholes he might have been hoping for. But at least it was an initial offer to move towards peaceful change, and a first glimmer of hope for Syrians. Outside Syria, people thought Assad had to go immediately, not in 2014, and if he didn't, the Syrian revolution would make him a thing of the past. Everyone laughed at Assad because they thought the war was won, and they didn't believe any kind of compromise, conversation or negotiation was necessary.

Former Finnish President Martti Ahtisaari, who was awarded the Nobel Peace Prize in 2008 for his work resolving many conflicts, came to a similar verdict. In 2012, he was involved in talks to end the Syrian civil war. Russia, as a major power backing the Syrian regime, had proposed that Assad should relinquish power once peace was agreed, but the US, France and UK had rejected this suggestion because they were so convinced that Assad's fall was imminent.[4]

It was a terrible error of judgement. With help from Iran and Russia, the regime in Syria regained the upper hand just a year later. Shiite militias and Russian warplanes gave it a military advantage, and in parallel an incredibly violent war was being waged by a regime against its own population. It became clear that the armed opposition couldn't withstand the Assad regime. Faced with this scenario, it was the West that started thinking aloud about potential peace negotiations. And now it was Assad who was laughing, as he no longer needed them.

The Syrian civil war continued until December 2024. UNICEF estimates that over half a million people have died in the course of the war, all because Assad was perpetuating his campaign of annihilating any dissent with the utmost brutality – but also because at decisive turning points, neither side was prepared to seek a path to peace from a position of strength.

Every concession is a betrayal

Lazaro Sumbeiywo, a Kenyan general who spent years facilitating peace talks during the Sudanese civil war, succinctly summed up the key problem with peace negotiations: 'Negotiations are the continuation of war in a different theater of operations.'[5] It's an almost brutally blunt statement that encapsulates all the difficulties that peace talks have to contend with. Negotiations don't mark the beginning of peace, and at first the battle is continued by other means – with words – and with an unspecified outcome. It is a coming together of bitter enemies who have committed the most savage crimes possible against each other, who deeply despise one another and who have vilified each other for years with every conceivable kind of hate speech. Every millimetre is fought for, every hint of diplomacy takes enormous effort, every friendly word is perceived as weakness and every concession as betrayal.

It's in this situation that opponents are supposed to sit down at a table and talk to each other. One side had their reasons for starting the war, knowing from the outset that the war would be barbaric, that it would cost many lives on their side as well as the other's, and that it would lead to economic suffering. And yet they still started the war. Why should they end it now, if they can envisage even the slightest chance of a military victory? People are usually only willing to negotiate if they see themselves in a position of weakness.

It is precisely at moments like this that we need a 'bigger person'; someone who is prepared to give in. Even in the war of aggression against Ukraine, there was a similar situation in the autumn of 2022 when a window for negotiations could have opened – there will be more about that towards the end of this book. It would have made for a more peaceful future for the world if the stronger military side in a war had also been the bigger person. In recent decades, research on peace has clearly demonstrated that peace negotiations usually only take place when a conflict is 'ripe' for it: when it's very damaging simultaneously for both sides, and when neither side has anything left to gain.

Both sides need to hurt

Here lies one of the toughest problems when it comes to a peaceful end to wars: both sides have to want peace at the same time. Only rarely is there a bigger person – a side that is prepared to give in. A warring party will not negotiate as long as it believes that it still has something to gain, or that it can at least get into a better negotiating position. This is a sad fact that has been shown time and time again in so many violent conflicts.

Until a war is 'ripe' for negotiations, any attempt at a diplomatic solution is doomed to fail. This concept of 'ripeness' was coined by William Zartman, a former peace researcher at Johns Hopkins University in Baltimore. He argues that at least two factors are needed to make negotiations possible: at a military level, a painful stalemate; and at a political level, a 'way out' – the suggestion of a potential solution.[6]

As long as one side believes it can achieve its goal without negotiations, it will refuse to negotiate, as the case of Syria shows, where first the West and then Assad rejected peace talks because they thought they were winning. The situation changes when a military stalemate arises: little is happening at the front; for a long time there are no breakthroughs by one side or the other; and subjectively neither side feels that there is still anything to gain. If this stalemate is really painful, the chances of peace talks increase. This 'pain' can come in many forms: a large death toll; the war costing so much money that the economy is being driven to ruin; or declining support from the population, which in turn endangers a leadership's position of power in their own country. If this applies to both sides in a conflict, we can call it a 'mutually hurting stalemate', which, according to William Zartman, is the crucial prerequisite for peace negotiations.

If the war threatens to cost more – financially and/or politically – than it can ultimately bring, it stops being worthwhile. Only when this is true for both sides will they start thinking about potential negotiated solutions. Zartman calls this a lose–lose situation: everyone loses, and no one wins. It's an extremely rational approach, and in fact most wars follow rational thinking: perhaps not always a rationality that we can understand from the outside, and certainly not one that we would consider to be right – but dictators and war criminals usually follow a certain logic, even if only to maintain their own power.

We can see what a mutually hurting stalemate looks like from the example of the Iran–Iraq War. In 1980, Saddam

What does it take to start peace negotiations?

Hussein's Iraq invaded its neighbour with the aim of resolving long-standing border conflicts by military means. At first, Iraq was able to conquer and occupy large areas of Iran. Then Iran increasingly went on the offensive, regaining all its land and in turn trying to invade Iraq. A war of attrition ensued, with both sides alternately seeming to make easy military gains every so often. It was an extremely brutal war. Iraq started to use chemical weapons and both sides bombed civilian residential areas in major cities. It was not until eight years – and over 500,000 deaths – later that both sides were finally ready for a ceasefire, after the realisation had sunk in that neither side could win and that both could only lose. The catastrophe in all this was that the 1988 ceasefire was agreed under roughly the same terms that had been proposed in 1982 – but before 1988, at least one side always thought it still had something to gain in the war.[7]

It was a similar story with the Bosnian War. In the summer of 1992, a vicious war between the various ethnic groups in Bosnia flared up. There were ethnically motivated mass murders of Muslim Bosnians, in particular the Srebrenica genocide in the summer of 1995, which is etched into the world's memory.

In 1995, the war was still being fought in all its brutality, but there was a certain balance of power and neither side was in a position to expect any major territorial gains. On top of this, Slobodan Milošević was no longer secure in his position as president of Serbia, as the sanctions set by the United Nations were putting a massive strain on the Serbian economy and his support among the population was crumbling fast. This scenario was a classic military stalemate that was damaging for both sides, and especially for the aggressor, Milošević. And it was precisely this situation that gave rise to the possibility of peace negotiations, which were concluded with the Dayton Agreement.

A brief aside: to this day, the legend persists that only the NATO air raids on Serbian positions made peace possible.

Former Swedish Prime Minister Carl Bildt, one of the chief negotiators of the Dayton Agreement, doesn't accept this interpretation. He noted in a background article that even the CIA later stated in no uncertain terms that 'militarily speaking, the practical effect of the NATO airstrikes was approximately zero' and that 'the evidence is even less convincing that the NATO air campaign brought the Bosnian Serbs to the negotiating table in Dayton.' In fact, according to the CIA memo, the Serbian side had accepted the negotiations before the NATO attack had even happened.[8]

A few years later the situation in Colombia, where a bloody civil war had been raging for many decades, was very similar to Bosnia, with various armed rebel groups, first and foremost the Fuerzas Armadas Revolucionarias de Colombia (FARC, or Revolutionary Armed Forces of Columbia). In the early 2000s, a mutually damaging stalemate had set in. FARC never had a realistic chance of military victory, and neither did the government, despite it had amassed an incredible amount of weapons. At the same time, the war against FARC came at a high political price for the Colombian rulers, as it came hand in hand with massive human rights violations. Arbitrary killings, expulsions, rapes and torture by the military, secret services or state-affiliated paramilitaries were ultimately not tolerated by the population of a country that prided itself on being the oldest democracy in Latin America. As a result, the conflict was eventually ripe for negotiations,[9] which in 2016 culminated in a peace agreement that is considered exemplary for many reasons – but we'll look at that in more detail in the next chapter.

The theory of the stalemate being painful for both sides sounds quite simple, but it's much more complicated in reality. It isn't enough simply to objectively assess that neither side has anything to gain. The warring parties themselves have to see it that way too. And that isn't straightforward, especially in war. At some point, one side starts to fall for its own propaganda and begins to believe in total victory, in a breakthrough in the next spring offensive, or in a revolt by the opponent's population. Sometimes it takes years for people to realise that in trench warfare at the front, nothing's really moving forward any longer and the news is only of losses.

The good news is that in a situation like this, there are many opportunities for peaceful intervention from the outside. Peace research rejects the concept that, in line with Zartman's model, other stakeholders simply have to wait for the time to be ripe before they can intervene supportively. On the contrary: third parties should look for ways to create a ripe time, at any stage of a conflict.[10] In the best-case scenario, economic sanctions might also significantly alter the warring parties' cost-benefit calculations.

This is where *war weariness* comes into play: when broad sections of the population can't bear the war any longer and stop supporting it, and when even among the soldiers a belief in victory starts to fade. It endangers the ruling elites' positions of power and can make a decisive contribution to the mutually damaging stalemate, paving the way for negotiations. Unfortunately, an awareness of this mechanism frequently determines how war is waged. Missile attacks on residential areas or on the power supply often have the precise aim of creating war weariness among the opponent's population.

The light at the end of the tunnel must be visible

Pain alone isn't enough, though; there also needs to be an understanding that a way forward is possible. At this point, it's not about clearly outlining the ultimate solution – this is practically never possible at the beginning of peace negotiations. We'll come back to that later. In fact, it's always surprising how the solutions look by the end of peace negotiations. However, the idea that there could be non-military solutions at all is an indispensable prerequisite for starting negotiations – and this is where the international community can actively intervene.

A good example, once again, is the peace negotiations at the end of the Bosnian War. Wolfgang Ischinger, the former chair of the Munich Security Conference, recently described these negotiations very vividly in an article in the German newspaper *Tagesspiegel*. With a view to possible peace solutions in the Russia–Ukraine war, he called for the West to rouse itself from its state of shock and prepare some potential peace solutions.[11] In 1995, before the negotiations in Dayton, the Americans had worked out a wide range of possible solutions and prepared for every conceivable eventuality. They had gone as far as drafting a constitution for Bosnia-Herzegovina, as well as agreements on arms control, and there were even some very specific ideas about a potential currency. Every detail had been thought of. Even though no one could have predicted how an agreement would ultimately look, the mere fact that possibilities were on the table and that a way forward was becoming visible contributed significantly to negotiations being set in motion. None of this foreshadowed the negotiations' outcome; it was just an assortment of potential options that offered a way forward in the early stages and that could facilitate the negotiations as they progressed.

The example of Bosnia teaches us an important lesson: even outsiders can make a significant contribution to the beginnings of peace negotiations, for example by outlining possible ways forward, by initiating an international debate on potential solutions or, as in the Dayton Agreement, by meticulously preparing the details. If a situation becomes 'ripe', this can provide the crucial trigger.

This is also true of the final step. When a conflict is ripe for negotiation, and when ways to step away from violence seem possible, the opportunity must be seized. This is when external mediators can step in, going back and forth between the warring parties and slowly but surely leading them across the finish line. And this is why all the mediation offers and shuttle diplomacy involved in the Ukraine war, from the Vatican to Brazil, are so important, even if they don't seem successful at first, since the situation isn't yet ripe for negotiations. Ultimately, they could prevent the right moment being missed.

Bigger player

The ripeness theory helps us understand when and why peace talks have become possible in many conflicts in the past. However, we should take care not to think of it as a simple formula: just wait until both sides are hurting and then trot off to the negotiating table. That would be far too passive an approach, and in many wars it would prolong the suffering for years. But there are other ways to intervene from the outside and pave the way towards a peaceful solution.

In the past, it has often been key for close allies of one of the warring parties to exert pressure on them to negotiate. Here, too, the Bosnian War is a prime example: both sides had countries they partnered with that agreed that the war should be stopped as quickly as possible. Russia, as a close ally of Serbia, played an important role in exerting pressure to bring Serbia to the negotiating table. Conversely, the same was true for the US and the EU as allies on the Bosnian side.

Situations like this, where a 'bigger player' exerts pressure – or at least actively uses persuasion – often occur in wars. Venezuela, for example, played a very important role in the much-praised Colombian civil war peace process by repeatedly putting pressure on the FARC rebel group to keep taking part in the negotiations, despite all the problems. If we apply this to the Russia–Ukraine war, the bigger player principle would mean convincing China to play a mediating role; but more on that later.

Stumbling blocks

War is always about passing the buck. The blame must always lie with the other side: we're the good guys, we want peace. This is why it's very rare for a warring party to reject negotiations outright and publicly. The easy way out is to formulate preconditions: we're ready to negotiate at any time, but only if you do this or that – if you withdraw behind this line or that line, if you permanently renounce your claim to this territory or that territory, if you recognise our financial demands, and so on.

Sometimes these might be fair and important demands, but however fair they may be, they can only ever be fulfilled as the result of negotiations, not as the starting point. In most cases, both sides have war objectives which are not usually compatible – if they were, the war would never have been waged in the first place. A solution to these conflicting goals can only be found through negotiations, and not before. So the simple basic rule applies: anyone who sets preconditions doesn't actually want to negotiate.

Another obstacle to negotiation is often the political propaganda that's been fed to each side's citizens. Each warring party constantly needs to secure its own population's approval, and so churns out incessant war propaganda for this purpose. This always involves demonising the opponent – monsters, child killers, criminals, maniacs. At some point this can cause real problems: how do I explain to my people that I want to negotiate with unscrupulous criminals?

There is also an objective problem here, because often both sides have in fact committed the worst imaginable war crimes and human rights violations. It goes against our common sense, and the international community's, to agree to enter into conversation with major criminals. But without talks there's no peace; without talks crimes, deaths and suffering on all sides are perpetuated. This is why we have to adhere to the principle of talking to all warring parties – every single one. Especially in civil wars, the question of whether it is acceptable to talk to 'terrorists' is repeatedly raised. In the Middle East conflict, this is a constant and recurring question that had very different answers in the past. In the 1990s, there was dialogue, and the Palestine Liberation Organisation (PLO) leader at that time, Yasser Arafat, went from being a 'terrorist' to a Nobel Peace Prize winner. 'Terrorist' is all too often just a battle cry used to discredit an opponent. Nelson Mandela was once classed as a 'terrorist' too, and thank goodness he was ultimately included in talks. The same goes for Northern Ireland, Colombia, Sudan and so many other civil wars where a peace deal was finally forged with former 'terrorists'. However, it is abundantly clear that after the unbelievably brutal massacre by Hamas on 7 October 2023, it is hard to imagine a genuine dialogue happening in the near future.

Keeping channels open

When I first heard about the Russian–Ukrainian grain deal, it made me optimistic. In the summer of 2022, in the midst of the war, Russia and Ukraine agreed on the safe passage of grain ships in the Black Sea. Two opponents talked to each other and found a common solution to a problem. I thought this could be the nucleus of further talks and perhaps even ultimately peace negotiations. Unfortunately, that was a mistake.

In a great many wars and conflicts, there are conversations about very practical things. The exchange of prisoners is a common example. This is because both sides have an interest in getting their own fighters back and in return ridding themselves of their prisoners, because they just cost money. It was similar with the grain deal. Both sides had, for very different reasons, an interest in the unhindered export of grain worldwide: Ukraine mainly for financial reasons; Russia not least because its allies in Africa and Asia were suffering from high grain prices.

Unfortunately, talks about issues of mutual interest tell us very little about the possibility of peace talks. However, they do keep communication channels open, and that in itself is worthwhile. But without the political will of key stakeholders, peace talks won't take place, no matter how many prisoners are exchanged.

There's plenty that can be done

This all sounds very sobering – and it probably is, if the warring parties are left to their own devices. On the other hand, it shows there are various ways to intervene from the outside and improve the chances of initiating peace negotiations. There's plenty that can be done by outsiders, by the EU, by individual governments. We've seen some very practical things that could significantly increase the likelihood of peace negotiations: countries that take on the 'bigger player' role, or are at least close allies, can exert considerable influence. Diplomatic efforts by third parties, such as the African Union or the Chinese special envoys in the Russia–Ukraine war, could be publicly supported and given more weight by other stakeholders. Outsiders can prepare potential ways forward out of a conflict. A warring party's cost-benefit analysis can also be influenced externally, either through sanctions, which make a stalemate increasingly costly, or through the promise of future cooperation. If a peace agreement holds the hope of more benefits than will be achieved by continuing the war, peace becomes much more likely.

More than anything else, though, there needs to be a long-term conviction, especially in the centres of power, that a strong position, however short-term, should be exploited immediately for potential peace negotiations. Never again should we be as sure of victory as we were in Syria in 2012.

2

PEACE NEGOTIATIONS

A good compromise is one that makes all sides equally unhappy[12]

When warring parties are finally ready to negotiate, there's still a long path to walk before lasting peace is secured, and it's often paved with setbacks, diversions and fresh starts. Academic reports and analyses on past peace negotiations of every kind provide a treasure trove of lessons and blueprints for all future conflicts. Even though every conflict is different and every solution is unique, there are always three things to keep in mind. First of all, resolving a conflict is a *long process*, and not everything can be resolved in an agreement. After the negotiations, the real work of implementation begins. Second, there is only a chance of lasting peace if *as many people as possible are involved*, rather than just two leaders hatching a plan behind closed doors. And third: *without trust, it won't work*, and it takes a long time to restore that trust after a war.

'Peace is not a product, but a process'[13]

Peace is a process, not an end result. This may sound like a rather banal aphorism to embroider and hang over the mantelpiece, but in fact it's the harsh reality of peace negotiations. The idea that warring parties sit down at a table, negotiate a compromise, sign it and then live happily ever after is just a naive pipe dream. In fact, negotiations often drag on for years, they might be suspended or even called off, violence can break out over and over again, and negotiators need to keep trying out new approaches. And when a document is finally signed off, it often takes years before all the aspects of the agreement are implemented.

This process – the long road to peace – does not end with peace negotiations, nor does it begin with them. There are often long phases of preliminary talks, when a wide variety of mediators sound out the parties involved in the war to see what might work. This was, and is, also true of the Russia–Ukraine war: again and again, new initiatives from Brazil, China, Switzerland and other countries are trying to find ways to work towards peace negotiations, using shuttle diplomacy between all the parties involved.

Even though many of these attempts fizzle out and most tend to take place behind closed doors, they are an important part of a peace process, as the cornerstones of potential talks can begin to crystallise from these initial ideas: who will be involved in negotiation?; Who will sit at the table, and who will mediate and moderate?; And what will be included in the talks: a ceasefire, a long-term detailed peace treaty, or something in between? Preliminary discussions like these are always important, but they are also often misused to prevent genuine negotiation. There might be talks about talks without any talk actually happening:[14] it's an opportunity for a side to present itself as the dove of peace without seriously seeking an end to the war.

The courage to leave gaps

As I said, peace is a long process. But it isn't just the time for preliminary talks and negotiations leading up to a ceremonial signing, but above all *the time afterwards*. In peace research, a peace treaty isn't seen as an end point, but as an intermediate step in a longer process. It's crucial for a peace treaty to ensure the process carries on. This realisation takes the pressure off negotiations; not everything has to be decided immediately, and some things can even be postponed until the implementation phase, in the hope that implementing an agreement's first steps will facilitate the following ones, or even make them possible in the first place.

Probably the world's most recognised authority on the time after a peace treaty is the Frenchman Jean Arnault. He has led a wide variety of peace processes for the UN and around twenty years ago he published a policy paper on the options and problems involved in implementing peace agreements, which is still considered a standard reference work today. For Arnault, a peace process is a 'gradual accommodation between the peace agreement and realities on the ground'.[15] It's only like this, with slow interaction with the real world, that lasting peace can be achieved.

A convincing example of this is the 2000 Burundi peace agreement, after 12 years of very bloody civil war. There were large gaps in this agreement, some armed groups weren't even at the table, and the negotiators failed to agree on several points. Despite all its shortcomings, the agreement was concluded to get the peace process off the ground. There was optimism that the first steps, unsteady though they may have been, would enable the next ones. As a result, almost all the opposition leaders were involved in the new government, in the hope that they'd be much more motivated to implement the agreement and that they'd drop some of their most extreme demands during the implementation period. The old, ethnically driven lines of conflict were in fact able to be pacified, even though now Burundi is once again suffering under an authoritarian regime and political violence is the order of the day.

Gaps in an agreement or 'constructive ambiguities'[16] are a popular stylistic device in negotiations to avoid a stalemate or even a breakdown. It often works, but these gaps mustn't relate to the key interests of the negotiating parties, Jean Arnault writes. If these interests are postponed until the later implementation phase without clear settlement, the warring parties in question won't support the agreement unreservedly and they'll keep the military option open.

There can also be problems the other way around: if an attempt is made to fully settle everything in the peace agreement, this can be too much to implement and can lead to the process failing. An example of this is the Guatemala Agreement, which looks wonderful on paper, but has barely been put into effect at all. After 36 years of civil war, peace was finally reached in 1996; we'll come back to this later. The peace agreement provided for far-reaching reforms to address the underlying causes of the conflict. Scarcely anything has been implemented to this day, and even the dictatorship's major perpetrators have gone unpunished.

Every peace agreement has a problem: it's a compromise. When I worked at the United Nations in New York, there was an amusing saying that a good compromise is one that makes all sides equally unhappy. In reality a compromise can become a problem that isn't that easy to solve; and the compromise must ultimately be supported by the general population. After years of violence and war propaganda, they are often unwilling to make concessions and abandon long-awaited goals.

So while the heads of governments or groups at the negotiating table are gradually distancing themselves from their most rigorous demands, broad public opinion tends to remain at the extremes. This is also compounded by the fact that the leaders of the warring parties lose their influence in society through a peace agreement. Fighting the enemy is no longer a unifying factor. After a war, according to Jean Arnault, bipolarity disappears. But it's replaced not by consensus but by multipolarity, because both sides go through a process of disintegration, resulting in divisions and polarisation. This makes it more difficult for a leadership to gain approval for a compromise among its supporters.

A seat at the table for all

Whether or not peace talks are successful depends very much on who's at the table and who isn't. The most obvious logic seems to be that peace negotiations are *political* conversations, and military expertise is not required: military forces have been waging the war, and now other people negotiate peace.

Experienced mediators, however, say that military leaders should be involved in negotiations. Jean Arnault, for example, argues that it's crucial to build trust between warring parties' military leaders, because they're the ones who will ultimately have to guarantee each other security and/or give up their weapons. In order to make this trust possible – trust both in their opponents and in the peace process itself – the military leaders should also have a seat at the table.

However, peace negotiations aren't just about the warring parties' leaders negotiating an agreement, laying down their arms and thereby ending the war. A war isn't merely two armies at war, but entire societies. Many people on both sides will have been affected by the war; they may have been victims or perpetrators, or often both. Hatred runs deep and wounds need time to heal if peace is to be given a chance.

This is why it should be the broadest possible cross-section of civil society sitting at the negotiating table. It's only if it's *their* peace treaty that people will uphold it on a day-to-day basis and call for its implementation. As a result, inclusivity has been very extensive in some cases of peace negotiations. In the Burundi peace process, for example, 19 political parties were involved. In Northern Ireland, special elections were held, and the ten most successful parties took part in negotiations.

Above all, though, women need to be involved. As a feminist, I'm pleased there is factual evidence that peace agreements are much more successful when women take a seat at the table. A research paper from 2014 statistically evaluated 156 peace agreements since the end of the Cold War and came to a clear conclusion: the probability of violence stopping within a year increased by 24.9 per cent when women participated in the negotiations. This was statistically significant and not just a coincidence. However, this improved success rate only occurred when women from the societies involved in the conflict sat at the negotiating table. Participation by women from third-party countries didn't alter the agreement's outcome. Nor is it effective to simply include a few passages on women's rights in a treaty – in this case, the likelihood of peace will actually decrease. A little rhetoric doesn't make peace, but active involvement by affected women does.[17]

This research is especially significant because it frees women's participation from merely a feel-good idea (nice gesture, but do we have to?). Still to this day, the inclusion of women is not a matter of course. Women are often excluded on the grounds that it isn't customary in some cultures to involve women in formal processes. In Northern Ireland, too, it looked like women were going to be left out. As a result, they founded their own women's party to run in the elections to secure a place at the negotiating table. They were successful, and women's involvement was certainly one element that contributed to peace in Northern Ireland.

It won't work without trust

When we sign a contract in civilian life, we trust that our counterpart will abide by it – or that a rules-based system can ensure this will happen. When we do our shopping we keep going to the greengrocer we trust because we've had years of experience of not being cheated there. And if there's any doubt, we can assert our rights in court. This is rarely necessary, though. It's usually best to conclude contracts on the basis of mutual trust – trust that doesn't even remotely exist at the beginning of peace negotiations.

As we've seen, 'negotiations are the continuation of war in a different theater of operations',[18] so where will the trust come from? Russia has just invaded a neighbour, flouting international law by breaking treaties. How could anyone trust the Kremlin to keep the promises that are crucial in peace negotiations? The same applies in civil wars. They are usually fought with even greater brutality and have significantly higher casualties among the civilian population than wars between two countries. Many conflicts begin because a section of society has lost confidence in the ruling system. And after many years of war, annihilation and loss, trust will be at an all-time low.

This is where the greatest difficulty lies in peace negotiations: how can trust be slowly rebuilt after all the violence and physical and mental war wounds? How can the weaker side be guaranteed not to ultimately lose everything? Without trust, it won't work. Jean Arnault, with his long-term experience as a mediator in internal conflicts, goes as far as saying that a peace agreement has no chance of success without fundamental trust between the parties involved; even the UN wouldn't be able to help.

At the beginning of negotiations, both sides often imply that their opponent is only sitting at the table for tactical reasons and has no real interest in a common solution. In a situation like this, Arnault says, there's no point in a mediator steering the talks towards concrete mutual interests. To begin with, confidence-building measures are essential. An example from Guatemala shows how these might look. In 1994, after over thirty years of civil war – which had its origins in a US-orchestrated coup, as we'll see in more detail in Chapter 12 – the UN sent a major mission to the country to review the human rights situation, with the Guatemalan government's approval. By allowing independent monitoring, the government sent an unmistakable signal to the rebels that it was serious about ending the prevailing state of civil war.

Conversely, the rebel organisations agreed to the UN mission providing technical support to the police and judicial system – the hated security apparatus they'd always fought against, which was responsible for large-scale human rights violations. By agreeing to this, the rebels were recognising the state's authority, in a roundabout way. These initial, cautious demonstrations of a desire for change from both sides bore fruit. A year later, the guerrillas indirectly participated in the national elections. The government refrained from repressing the candidates associated with them and the peace process was able to take its course. Ultimately, a comprehensive peace agreement was reached (although, for a variety of reasons, many of its elements weren't implemented).

Even before negotiations begin, confidence-building measures can help pave the way for future conflict resolution between two nations. For example, there have been border conflicts between Guatemala and Belize since colonial times. At the end of the 1990s, this escalated to the point that troops gathered on both sides of the border. At that point, the Organization of American States (OAS) – the association of all the nations on the continent – intervened, initiating a comprehensive series of measures to slowly rebuild trust between the two states, including close cooperation in the event of natural disasters, direct contact between local communities and between the military forces, and even a joint campaign against illegal activities in the border region. The OAS monitored it all. In the end, an escalation of the conflict was avoided, and now determining the line the border takes is in the hands of the International Court of Justice.[19]

Onions and other needs

In 2017, I took part in a training course organised by the German Federal Foreign Office, in which members of parliament could become familiar with the basic principles of international peace mediation. The German government set it up as part of their goal to provide greater support for future peace processes; the idea was to build up expertise among German politicians. The training was some of the best I've ever come across, and some highly experienced mediators from the UN shared their experiences in some of the most diverse peace efforts around the world.

What we learned from the course was that peace talks follow classic negotiation models, just like the ones in the free market economy. There are entire manuals and countless seminars on business negotiation strategies and tactics, and many of these can also be applied to peace processes. For example, there's the onion model, which assumes that there's a difference between a negotiating party's visible stances at surface level and the core needs at the heart of their thinking. The model is based on three layers: on the outside, demands; underneath, concerns; and in the centre, the essentials.

The onion's outer layer is what we see: the demands made publicly, the things that seem to be a negotiating party's goals. And sometimes they are. Not every demand is just a tactical distraction; often they're meant to be taken seriously. But they don't necessarily get to the essence of the negotiators' interests.

Their actual interests, in other words what the respective parties really want, are often not revealed immediately. It's all part of the negotiation tactics. This is where the first major mediation task lies – in slowly but surely peeling away the public demands layer by layer and understanding what interests lie beneath them, and what the actual negotiation goal is.

But there's more to it than that, as the various parties' interests often contradict each other, and compromises have to be made. Here we come to the third and final layer, to the heart of the compromise: each side's fundamental requirements, things that they must have, no matter what, demands that they cannot do without, under any circumstances. The great art of mediation and peacemaking lies in working out each side's absolutely essential requirements and forging a solution from them.

At the same time, we have to realise that before negotiations begin, even the parties themselves might not be sure what they can and cannot do without. Who would have thought there could be a peace agreement in Northern Ireland without a territorial change and without a merger with the Republic of Ireland? Ultimately, the heart of the solution lay in the social issue: in the status of the Northern Irish Catholic population. At the end of this chapter, we'll look into the Northern Irish background in more detail, but for now, belonging to the Republic of Ireland was without doubt a big interest, but it didn't turn out to be the Catholic side's key, indispensable need in negotiations.

The fundamental concerns that come to the surface in peace negotiations are sometimes bizarre. In Bosnia, for example, talks were in danger of failing because there was no name for the Serb entity in Bosnia that was acceptable to all sides – until they eventually agreed on 'Republika Srpska'. It sounds absurd, but according to Swedish negotiator Carl Bildt, this was in fact one of the most important breakthroughs during negotiations.[20] It was probably such a difficult question because the name touched on the question of identity, one of the parties' key needs in the Bosnian War.

Don't talk about the potential outcome too soon

A significant insight from past peace negotiations is that what a solution will ultimately include is completely unknown at the beginning. It has to be an open-ended process if it's going to have any chance of success at all. This is why the Austrian Wolfgang Sporrer, who has attended numerous negotiations on behalf of the Organization for Security and Co-operation in Europe (OSCE), warns against even discussing potential outcomes for Ukraine in advance: 'All conceivable end scenarios will be rejected at this point,' he writes.[21]

We certainly shouldn't presume to be able to predict what an unconditional prerequisite for peace between Ukraine and Russia should be. Constantly maintaining that there can't be any kind of peace because both Moscow and Kyiv have enshrined a claim to the Donbas region in their constitutions is also nonsense. Ireland has shown us this: the Irish constitution also stipulated that the entire island was its territory. Although this claim to Northern Ireland had constitutional status, it wasn't ultimately inalienable. As part of the peace process, Ireland abandoned the claim and held a referendum to amend its constitution.

Security guarantees

One of the most difficult points in peace processes – both in negotiations and, in the following years, during implementation – is the issue of security, especially when mutual trust is still fragile. Particularly in the aftermath of civil wars, the problem of security can be a major one. On the one hand, the state will insist on its monopoly on the use of force, which means the rebel groups will have to give up their weapons and integrate into civil society. On the other hand, weapons are the only pawn the rebels have. They will only consent to being disarmed if they can be sure the other side will honour their promises afterwards. The solution, Jean Arnault writes, is to carry across the balance of power that made peace negotiations possible into the implementation phase. Any imbalances must be foreseen and corrected; this is the only way to ensure that both sides, including the weaker one in negotiations, adhere to the agreement.

A trade-off of this kind could be 'power sharing', in other words the participation of all the warring parties in the future government. According to Jean Arnault, power sharing is also really important because rebel groups in particular often overestimate their influence and wouldn't be able to fulfil their tasks under the agreement without participation in the future government. Weaker parties are more likely to stick with it if they're included in the new government, and they would then have power to lose if they were to withdraw from the agreement, Arnault says.

The concept of security has evolved significantly in the last 30 years, and it no longer just means safety from violence.

Today, the broad term 'human security' is increasingly being used. In 2012, the UN General Assembly defined human security as 'the right of people to live in freedom and dignity, free from poverty and despair [...] Human security recognizes the interlinkages between peace, development and human rights, and equally considers civil, political, economic, social and cultural rights.'[22] This is an important aspect of peace processes, because they will ultimately only succeed if people can be guaranteed security from exploitation and (state) violence.

The concept of human security is closely related to the idea of 'positive peace' developed by the Norwegian peace researcher Johan Galtung over fifty years ago. It comes from the realisation that peace is far more than merely the absence of war. Positive peace, according to Galtung, includes social and economic justice as well as an absence of structural violence; only when the potential causes of war have been eliminated can there genuinely be peace.

It always refers to the step beyond the actual end of war: the underlying causes need to be addressed, and they are mainly rooted in social issues and democratic freedoms. Unjust ownership structures or unclear land rights, a lack of equality, arbitrariness, oppression and exploitation are incompatible with sustainable peace. Peace is definitely much more than the absence of war – and yet the fact that the guns have been put down and no one's being shot any more is in itself a virtue. The tension between a quick end to the killing and true peace is a difficult stage that is never easy to resolve. This is the case for Ukraine as well: there's often a world of difference between weapons falling silent and a 'just peace'.

The double-edged role of ceasefires

At first glance, a ceasefire seems like a good thing: the guns are put to one side, people are no longer being killed, and humanitarian corridors are being opened. With the Gaza war following the massacre by Hamas on 7 October 2023, calls for a truce have been repeated around the world to give the civilian population in Gaza some respite, to enable aid deliveries and to exchange hostages for prisoners. It happened just once, at the end of November 2023, and after that, no attempt to mediate for a renewed ceasefire came to anything for months on end. For people in an acutely war-torn region who don't know if they'll still be alive tomorrow, a truce or a ceasefire is a blessing.

Ceasefires can also defuse conflicts in the long term, sometimes even for decades. Cyprus is an example of this; there has been no real peace treaty there for decades, and the north of the country is still occupied by Turkish troops, but the ceasefire is maintained; it has been a long time since shots have been fired; and, with the UN's help, minor conflicts are quickly defused.

The ceasefire in Korea isn't quite as effective. The conflict hasn't been defused at all to date, and there is constant sabre-rattling, missile tests and nuclear threats. And yet, since 1953, the ceasefire has managed to prevent a 'hot war' between North and South Korea. Today, the Korean War has almost completely disappeared from public consciousness, but at the time it took the world to the brink of nuclear war and claimed four million lives in just three years between 1950 and 1953. It began with an attack by the north on the south, and within a year the front shifted down to the far south before moving north again, only for a horrific war of attrition to continue along the old border in 1951. Here, too, it took another two years of gruesome war before there was finally a ceasefire agreement and a demilitarised zone along the border.[23] To this day, no peace treaty exists, and the constant threatening gestures from North Korea do not give an impression of peace at all; yet this ceasefire, which has lasted for over seventy years, has certainly saved many lives and has enabled South Korea – only South Korea – to develop.

Here's a brief aside on terminology: there is no clear distinction between a truce and a ceasefire. As a rule, a *truce* is used to refer to a brief interruption of hostilities, usually only verbally agreed and often with a very specific purpose, such as for humanitarian aid, and a precise time limit. What was agreed between Israel and Hamas in November 2023 and spring 2024 were truces of this kind, only for a few days and with the specific aim of exchanging prisoners and supplying aid. A *ceasefire*, on the other hand, is more likely to be a contractual agreement between the warring parties not to engage in hostilities for a longer period of time. However, the lines between these terms are fluid; even between Israel and Hamas negotiations took weeks or even months and all the conditions were recorded in detail, so there was also a contractual basis in this case, but conversely it was only for a short period of time with a concrete goal, which is why both terms were used in the media.

Even though a ceasefire is, of course, very desirable from the point of view of the people in the areas being fought over, it's viewed critically in peace research, for very different reasons. Simply announcing publicly that from tomorrow you won't shoot any more will scarcely change a thing in most situations. One wrong shot at the wrong time, one misunderstanding, one small renegade unit, and bang goes the ceasefire. Genuine reliability, including the security to plan humanitarian aid, and peace for the civilian population on the ground, can only be achieved if the ceasefire is based on a negotiated agreement that sets out mechanisms to monitor it as well as communication channels to clear up misunderstandings.

Another problem with ceasefires is that fighting can escalate shortly beforehand, because each side wants to shift the balance of power or territory as much as possible in its own favour to improve its own negotiating position for forthcoming talks. An imminent ceasefire could therefore have extremely threatening consequences for people in the affected areas.

Sabine Kurtenbach of the German Institute for Global and Area Studies (GIGA) in Hamburg has spent many years researching the civil war in Colombia and says that 'for all intents and purposes ceasefires are equivocal and in many cases problematic'.[24] In Colombia, a comprehensive ceasefire in the late 1990s was used by both sides to regroup. After that, violence erupted on an unprecedented scale, even for Colombia. It's a mistake to think that violence always ends with a ceasefire, according to Sabine Kurtenbach; sometimes the violence only shifts and the civilian population often bears the brunt. There were no ceasefires in place during the negotiations in Colombia between 2012 and 2016. This led to some crises in the process, as both sides continued to carry out spectacular campaigns against each other. Nevertheless, the process was supported by both sides so the appalling experience of the previous ceasefire wouldn't be repeated – and also to exert pressure in the talks.[25]

Ceasefires can even make peace negotiations more difficult. When the guns fall silent, a military stalemate – a state of deadlock with heavy losses – is no longer as damaging and the will to engage in serious negotiations drops dramatically. In recent peace research, the latest thinking is that ceasefires can be agreed at the beginning of peace negotiations, but that they should have a time limit so that pressure is maintained in negotiations.[26] The United Nations makes a distinction between temporary and permanent ceasefires. An example of this is the war between Ethiopia and Eritrea. A temporary truce was agreed in 2000 in order to put a short-term freeze on the conflict, buying some time to negotiate a comprehensive ceasefire.[27]

Two examples: trials and tribulations on the path to peace

In the Philippines, peace negotiations lasted no less than 17 years until an agreement was reached in 2014. The peace researcher Kristian Herbolzheimer attended this process for several years and documented it in detail.[28] Since 1969, a civil war had been raging on Mindanao, the southernmost island of the Philippines, between the local Muslim population and the deeply Catholic country's central government. It was not until 1997 that serious peace negotiations began.

Talks were practically on the verge of collapse three times, in 2000, 2003 and 2008. Each time, however, the parties found a way to breathe life back into the process. The first time, the stalemate was overcome by bringing in neighbouring Malaysia as a mediator. The second time, an international group was set up to monitor the ceasefire. In 2009, this group was expanded again.

The conflict was ultimately resolved primarily by establishing a new self-governing region called Bangsamoro in the predominantly Muslim area. The agreement is very complex and governs details such as the transition processes and financial issues. One of the biggest challenges was 'normalisation', the transition from a civil war infrastructure to peaceful communities. This included disarming and demobilising fighters and clarifying security issues. There were agreements on socio-economic measures and on the expansion of education and healthcare. Amnesties were granted to members of the armed groups if no serious crimes had been committed, and a programme was set up to help people come to terms with the past, which we'll return to in the next chapter.

The issue of security was key to the negotiations. On the one hand, the state security apparatus was reformed; on the other, rebel army members and their weapons were put on a register. The rebels agreed to complete disarmament, but in a gradual process. Initially, the weapons were kept under the joint control of the government and former rebels, with the help of international coordination.

The agreement's relative success depended on an understanding from both sides that it had to have the support of the respective populations. To guarantee the people's involvement and consent – to make it *their* peace agreement – several hundred thousand rebel supporters were informed about the negotiations' progress at public events to ensure support for the agreement's provisions.

My second example of difficult and protracted peace negotiations is Northern Ireland, where a peace agreement, signed on Good Friday 1998, still stands today and is highly regarded around the world as a blueprint for successful negotiations. For anyone who thinks of Guinness when Ireland comes to mind and who isn't so familiar with the civil war, the Emerald Isle was part of Great Britain for many centuries. It wasn't until 1922 that Ireland became independent, but the northern, predominantly Protestant part of the island remained a part of the United Kingdom. This secession from Northern Ireland was never accepted by the Irish Catholic population in the rest of the island. A rejection of all things British was very deep-seated among Irish Catholics, fuelled by centuries of oppression and poverty. The Great Famine of 1845, in which one million people died in Ireland and two million emigrated, is to this day deeply etched in the collective memory. After Ireland's independence in 1922, a decades-long civil war developed in Northern Ireland, with the Irish Republican Army (IRA) fighting against British occupation. The conflict also had religious aspects: Catholic Ireland against Protestants of British descent.

Over the decades, several attempts to forge a peace process failed, until in 1993 the first viable preliminary talks were held between the two warring parties in Northern Ireland and between the London and Dublin governments. These preliminary talks paved the way for a unilateral ceasefire by the IRA in August 1994, joined shortly afterwards by the armed Protestant groups. Negotiations began in 1995.

Corinna Hauswedell, one of Germany's most renowned peace researchers, has published some comprehensive analyses of the Northern Ireland conflict.[29] She emphasises that the

United States actively participating in the peace process was of key importance. The US sent George Mitchell, a high-ranking politician, as a mediator. To this day, his contribution is considered crucial for the peace negotiations' success. There was also a major investment campaign from US firms, creating a considerable number of industrial jobs in Northern Ireland between 1993 and 1998.

Corinna Hauswedell writes that 'disarmament in people's minds' was an important prerequisite for the peace process. It wasn't merely a military confrontation – the IRA against the British – but a centuries-long conflict that was 'over-ideologised' and 'conducted with ideological bandages and blinkers on both sides'. In a situation like that, there is no easy, pragmatic way to work together or at least co-exist peacefully. The hatred is too deep, and the demarcation is omnipresent.

Here's a quick anecdote: once when I was on a hike with Irish friends in the heart of the Republic of Ireland, we asked an old farmer for directions. A friendly conversation developed. As we walked off, one of my Irish friends muttered to herself, 'Church of England' – in other words, a descendant of British immigrants, possibly hundreds of years ago, but still 'Church of England': not Irish, not Catholic, not 'one of us' to my friend; but instead an occupier, colonialist and co-perpetrator of the 1845 Great Famine; 'Church of England' was used as a completely normal, everyday classification by a progressive person in 2018, 20 years after the Good Friday Agreement. It was only then that I realised how much time mental disarmament takes in people's hearts and minds and how long it takes to achieve real peace.

This is something a peace agreement such as the Good Friday Agreement cannot achieve. It was about *material disarmament*. In Ireland, as always, security was one of the most difficult issues in the peace process and almost led to its failure on several occasions. It started with the British side announcing it would only negotiate with the groups that had surrendered their weapons. In other words, it made both a ceasefire, which had been in place since 1994, and the other side's total and immediate disarmament, a precondition for negotiations. The US mediator Mitchell clearly rejected this and established the principle that armed groups would be allowed to negotiate without surrendering their weapons – but only as long as they complied with the ceasefire.[30] As a result, over the course of the following few years, there was occasionally a negotiating party absent from the table because they had broken the ceasefire. Towards the end, however, in the days running up to Easter 1998, everyone was involved, and negotiations were successfully concluded.

The security issue was settled in the agreement as follows: the entire police force, which was almost exclusively made up of Protestants before the peace agreement, was to be restructured to provide Catholics with a sense of genuine security. On the other side, the IRA gradually surrendered its weapons. What was achieved here corresponds to what Corinna Hauswedell describes as 'an understanding of reciprocity, the gradual establishment of a common, non-partisan understanding of security'. A further difficulty was the excessive ideological and symbolic weight that IRA weapons carried for both sides: to the IRA, weapons were the symbol of the Irish struggle for freedom; to the British, they were a symbol of terror. It was only when, as a result of the Good Friday Agreement, the IRA-affiliated Sinn Féin party did exceptionally well in elections that the IRA agreed to disarm. This was done, Hauswedell said, 'from a position of strength and was no longer associated with defeat or submission in the republican consciousness'.

Involvement of the general population in Northern Ireland was achieved through two mechanisms. For one thing, the best possible inclusivity at the negotiating table had already been ensured through the ten strongest parties participating; and for another, the Good Friday Agreement would be voted on in a referendum in May 1998, to unite as many people as possible behind the peace agreement.

All these examples from past peace negotiations, from Korea to Iran and Iraq, from the Philippines to Bosnia and Northern Ireland, teach us two things above all: it's possible; and it's complicated.

Yes, it is possible to fight and negotiate at the same time. Even in seemingly hopeless situations, it's still possible to set the first steps towards a peaceful solution in motion, in civil wars as well as wars between nations. Most examples of negotiated solutions come from civil wars. This is simply because the number of wars between nations has decreased significantly since the Second World War, and the vast majority of violent conflicts have been domestic since then. But not all: since the end of the Second World War, almost twenty wars between two or more countries, from small border skirmishes such as in Guatemala and Belize to the really big conflicts in Korea, between Iran and Iraq or between India and Pakistan, have been placated with negotiations.[31]

But, of course, negotiated solutions are complicated. Convinced though I am that words, not weapons, are the only path to a secure, lasting peace, this isn't an easy path. Setbacks are inevitable; it can take years, and the real work starts with a peace treaty. But if the alternative is permanent war and endless destruction, death and suffering, we must do everything in our power to try to find a peaceful negotiated solution and to support it from the outside, with all our resources.

3

CLOSING THE WOUNDS: JUSTICE FOR THE VICTIMS

When a war ends, a woman's fight begins!

A time after a war is a time before a war, if the crimes of the past aren't dealt with and the victims aren't adequately compensated, where possible, and if the underlying causes of the war aren't eliminated and if the war wounds have no chance of healing. In peace research, the process of coming to terms with events after a war is called 'transitional justice'. It can best be described as dealing with the past. Transitional justice now plays a key part in negotiating peace agreements and resolving conflicts in the long term: without working thoroughly through the past, conflicts will continue to smoulder and can break out over and over again. I learned what this can look like in practice from Lian Gogali, a peace activist from Indonesia. Gogali, the founder and director of Institut Mosintuwu, which is dedicated to peacebuilding in the Poso region, initiated a reconciliation process there many years ago and has an impressive track record.

'You killed my husband!'[32]
The story began at Christmas 1998 in the small town of Poso in the centre of the Indonesian island of Sulawesi. A local dispute developed into a civil war, fought on religious grounds, throughout the region. Christian and Muslim groups

fought each other extremely violently, and deaths were rife. According to Lian Gogali, there were rarely any religious conflicts in Poso's history before then. Before the civil war broke out, Christianity and Islam were both very moderate there. One imam was even married to a Christian woman, and the community generally took this in its stride. People lived side by side in peace. The unwritten rule was always that the mayor would come from one religious group, and the deputy from the other.

The fact that a local dispute between two youth gangs could turn into a religious war had nothing to do with power or money. Elections were imminent. The incumbent mayor was in danger of being voted out of office because of a corruption scandal and he exploited religion to save his job. A lot of money was at stake: six months earlier, the long-time Indonesian dictator Suharto had been forced to abdicate, and the regions had become extensively autonomous, and were able to choose for themselves how investments were made. There are extensive gold and nickel deposits in Poso, so a corrupt politician in the mayor's office can make a lot of money very quickly.

The regional conflict was also fuelled by nationwide developments. The military had lost a massive amount of influence after Suharto's fall and saw the conflict in Sulawesi as an opportunity for a new role. In the years that ensued, there was no end to the violence. Entire villages were burned to the ground, and more than a third of the region's population fled. In 2001, there was a peace agreement of sorts, but organised groups continued to carry out terrorist attacks in the area.

Lian Gogali grew up in Poso, leaving the island to study. She only returned for her master's dissertation; she wanted to conduct interviews with women in Poso to collect and record their memories of the time when the civil war was going on. The academic project quickly turned into political work. She began to realise that poorer women in particular were not being heard. There was no space in the prevailing discourse for their stories. They had almost lost their own memories, Gogali says. It was at this point that she started coordinating the women. 'When a war ends, the women's fight begins,' she says.

Gogali went from door to door, talking to working women and housewives, primarily women with little education. These women had very direct experience of the war; they had had to flee into the jungle and survive there for a long time. After the war, they had no voice, and no representative group. With them, Gogali developed the concept of peace schools, where women could share their stories. To start with, many women came to vent their anger: 'You killed my husband!' All the women saw themselves as victims, even if their husbands had been among the perpetrators in the war. Then they met women from the other side, who were also victims, but whose husbands had been among the other side's perpetrators.

On this basis, the women of Poso were able to develop an understanding that every single one of them had experienced losses. Remembrance work, which acknowledges the diversity of memories and makes them comprehensible, is genuine peace work. It results in solidarity and, above all, a future. The women of Poso no longer needed to remain stuck in the past and in their losses; they could talk about the future again. And they could begin to create one.

When the peace schools began in 2009, the various religious groups in Poso were still very separate as a result of the civil war; there were villages that were purely Muslim or purely Christian, which was very different from the past. People were afraid of each other. So many had been killed in the name of religion. Today, adherents of each religion are generally living together in peace once again, and division is slowly dying out – an achievement that the peace schools and recognition of mutual violations certainly played a major part in.

The work is far from over, though: even now there are still politicians who aren't afraid to use religion among the communities in Poso for their own financial interests. There is a large industrial area in the region, known mainly for its nickel mining. The nickel goes to be processed in Grünheide in the German state of Brandenburg, at the Tesla factory. There is a plan to build a dam to supply electricity to Poso's industrial area; the owner of the company involved is Indonesia's former vice-president, who shamelessly uses the old traumas to push the project through. When residents protest that they're likely to lose their land because of the dam, they are labelled as Christians trying to incite unrest, just like in the old days. The region, which was returning to peaceful coexistence, is once again being stirred up. 'We're paying the price here for the nickel that's used in your cars,' says Lian Gogali.

Dealing with the past: transitional justice

The Poso peace schools' work is one of many examples worldwide of how coming to terms with the past effectively can help to defuse conflicts and make lasting peace possible, but the concept of transitional justice originated in a completely different context: in Latin America in the 1990s, after dictatorships in many countries came to an end. Coming to terms with the injustices that had been committed and prosecuting those responsible were important steps in the transition to democracy in Central and South American countries.

The idea then became known internationally through South Africa. After the end of apartheid, the new president, Nelson Mandela, established the Truth and Reconciliation Commission (TRC) in 1996. It became world-famous as an example of how to organise a peaceful transition to a new form of society so that old wounds could be closed. Instead of a victor's justice and a fresh sense of injustice from new massacres of the former perpetrators came crime investigation and dialogue between groups of the population.

The concept of transitional justice originated from a focus on prosecuting perpetrators for their crimes, based on the Nuremberg trials of the Nazi regime's leading figures in

1945–1946. Since then, it has become clear that while legal proceedings are an important component of reconciliation work they are not enough on their own. However, court proceedings are usually perceived as victor's justice by some parts of society, and they can even make genuine reconciliation work more difficult. 'You killed my husband' can either be expressed woman to woman in a protected space and lead to both acknowledging their simultaneous roles as members of a community of perpetrators and victims, or 'You killed my husband' can be played out in court, with a final verdict that sets out the perpetrators' and victims' roles in black and white. It's difficult to carry out both mutual remembrance work and criminal justice at the same time.

Since it first became a concept, transitional justice has undergone some changes and now works best as a multi-pronged approach, as Natascha Zupan from the renowned Berghof Foundation reports.[33] She is one of the most accomplished experts on the subject and has published widely on the potential and limits of transitional justice. While the concept had its origins in the democratic upheaval of societies after dictatorship or the apartheid regime, since the end of the 1990s it has also played an important role in peace processes to transform post-war societies peacefully, as in Lian Gogali's example in Indonesia.

The UN is also doing a lot of work in this area; it has a group of experts who are consulted in peace processes all over the world to ensure that issues of reconciliation and new justice are included from the outset when a peace agreement is being negotiated. In 2023, the UN published a comprehensive framework document on this subject, formulating four key goals for transitional justice: *establishing truth*; *justice*; *reparations*; and *preventing a relapse* into civil war or dictatorship.[34]

The means used to prevent a repetition of atrocities depends enormously on the character of the previous injustice. After dictatorships, a reform of the judicial and security systems definitely forms part of this, as they are usually a dictatorship's key cornerstones. To be sure history won't be repeated, functionaries who had a significant role in the injustice – either in a dictatorship or in a civil war – must, whatever happens, leave their jobs. But informal steps are also key. Especially after a civil war, it is crucial to reconcile the divided society, build new trust and repair any injustices.

Above all, however, the conflict's underlying causes must be addressed. These are often social injustices, and resolving them can be particularly complex, as they often touch the foundations of a society organised in line with capitalism. A pivotal cause of the civil war in Colombia, for example, was a lack of land rights for poor farming families. As a result, a land reform was agreed in the peace process, with three million hectares being distributed to smallholders: land that the state was to buy from the landowners in a mutually agreed process. In this way, and only in this way, one cause of the war could be eliminated without simultaneously creating a new one through expropriation. It was an acclaimed, very tangible attempt to prevent a repetition of the violent conflict.

International jurisdiction

Even if transitional justice is now primarily about dealing with the past, a legal reappraisal of past crimes is essential to put an end to impunity, too. Impunity is a very big problem, because if perpetrators expect to get away scot-free from the outset, they will commit the worst crimes without restraint. Only when impunity comes to an end can violence be contained.

However, in wars or civil wars, the national justice system is often unwilling or unable to prosecute crimes from within its own ranks. And after a conflict, there is always the danger that a nation's jurisdiction will be perceived by one side as victor's justice. This is why international jurisdiction exists: to investigate the most serious crimes and bring the perpetrators to justice.

The two most significant international courts are the International Court of Justice and the International Criminal Court. They may sound similar, and both are based in The Hague, but they are two completely different courts – both of which regularly make headlines.[35]

Let's begin with the International Court of Justice (ICJ). It's been around since 1945, since the UN was founded, and it is a body of the UN, just like the UN Security Council, for example. Here, nations can take other nations to court, but not individuals. The ICJ also gives legal opinions when requested by a country, or by the UN. Many cases dealt with by the ICJ revolve around border disputes, for example. In cases like these, the court has always represented a very important way to resolve conflicts peacefully: throughout history, border disputes have led to major wars on many occasions. However, the ICJ has more often been in the news because of legal decisions of great political significance; for example a 2004 opinion in which the ICJ declared the Israeli wall being built on occupied territory in the West Bank to be illegal. In 1996, the court held that any threat of nuclear weapons, let alone their use, was contrary to international law.

Most recently, the ICJ was once again the focus of world attention when South Africa filed a lawsuit against Israel at the end of 2023 amid fears of genocide in the Gaza Strip. The court hasn't yet taken a position on the accusation of genocide – it will certainly be two or more years before this happens – but in an emergency decision, it ruled that Israel had to take various measures immediately to prevent genocide.[36] In this case, South Africa was explicitly concerned not just about an assessment of whether or not a genocide was being committed, but above all with preventing a potential genocide.

The ICJ has an important legislative function, but it cannot prosecute individual perpetrators. This is the purpose for which the International Criminal Court (ICC) was founded in 1998. It isn't an organ of the UN but was founded as a result of an international treaty, the Rome Statute. Over 120 countries are now party to it. Unfortunately, the usual suspects are not among them: Russia, the US and China still refuse to open themselves up to international jurisdiction.

The ICC has its roots in the International Criminal Tribunal for the Former Yugoslavia, established by the UN Security Council in 1993 in the light of the most serious human rights crimes in the wars there, with the task of bringing the biggest perpetrators on all sides to justice. The court has been a great success, indicting over 160 suspects and convicting over 80, including key perpetrators such as the former president of Serbia, Slobodan Milošević. From a transitional justice point of view, the Yugoslavia tribunal was a vital factor in sending out a clear signal: no one who commits war crimes should go unpunished – anyone who does so now can be prosecuted in the future.

The ICC was founded in 1998 to send out this signal for future wars, and it has been doing good work ever since. In March 2023, for example, the ICC issued an arrest warrant for Vladimir Putin for deporting Ukrainian children to Russia. And in January 2024, relatives of victims of the Hamas massacre of 7 October 2023 turned to the ICC to ensure that Hamas perpetrators would be prosecuted.

Great though the ICC is as an institution, it is, of course, very limited in its powers and it can only prosecute a fraction of all war crimes. The 80 and more convictions for crimes committed in the Yugoslav wars aren't even the tip of the iceberg. However, there is a very unusual solution to this problem, with a grandiose name: the 'universal jurisdiction principle'. The idea behind it is much simpler: a nation can prosecute crimes under international law, even if it isn't directly affected by them in any way, in other words if neither its citizens nor its own territory are affected. In Germany, this is laid down in the law called the Völkerstrafgesetzbuch (international criminal code), which is fundamentally based on the ICC's Rome Statute.

This means that proceedings against torturers and genocides in other countries can be conducted in Germany as well as elsewhere. One example is what was known as the Al-Khatib trial at the Higher Regional Court in Koblenz.[37] Two Syrian intelligence officers responsible for inconceivable atrocities in a Syrian torture prison, who had moved to Germany, were charged. They were ultimately sentenced, one of them to life imprisonment in a German prison, with the help of the universal jurisdiction principle. Their victims were able to testify before the court as witnesses and in some cases also appeared as private prosecutors. There's no impunity for anyone, anywhere in the world: the Al-Khatib trial was a wonderful example of this.

A voice for the victims

Important as the investigation of war crimes may be, it has a fundamental problem in terms of transitional justice: court proceedings deal primarily with the perpetrators. Victims may appear as witnesses, but the process isn't really about their story. This was also one of the criticisms of the South African Truth and Reconciliation Commission, where perpetrators, in particular, could describe their version of the truth while many other truths remained unheard.

Genuine reconciliation is only possible if victims are also given a voice. There are often victims on several sides of a conflict. In Poso, for example, the women were victims but came from families, villages or religious communities where perpetrators were also living. But even if the different groups were enemies, they had one thing in common: the civil war had made victims of them all. Many of them lost loved ones and experienced violence themselves. This is the focal point where working with victims can lead to true reconciliation.

Organisations worldwide try to give victims a voice to break the endless spiral of violence and counter-violence. One of them in particular stands out because it took the principle of 'giving victims a voice' very literally. In 2009, while Lian Gogali was setting up her peace schools in Indonesia, several young Afghans founded the Afghanistan Human Rights and Democracy Organisation (AHRDO) in Kabul, 10,000 kilometres away. It mainly involved people who were injured or bereaved by the war in Afghanistan, a war that devastated the country for many decades, starting with the invasion by the Soviet Union in 1979, and with so many fluctuating coalitions, warlords and militias that many people in Afghanistan saw each other as deeply hostile. But then they realised that they all had something fundamental in common: they were victims. There is scarcely a family in Afghanistan who hasn't suffered the violent death of at least one of its members. And that's exactly what connects them: their grief for loved ones, and living in constant fear.

The method chosen by AHRDO to let the victims' stories be heard was theatre. They developed plays about the violence and suffering of war, not at their desks or with professional actors, but with the people affected, who ended up on stage. AHRDO received support from bodies including the German organisation Medico International, which combines concrete humanitarian aid with long-term political work in many of its projects. Hadi Marifat, one of the founders of AHRDO, described the principle of this work in an interview with Medico: 'The exercises and games create an atmosphere of trust, so that people are ultimately willing to share their stories and problems. This is very important in a country where a long history of wars and conflicts has permanently destroyed the foundation of trust.'[38]

AHRDO followed a simple principle: telling the story of the war in Afghanistan means drawing out the victims' stories rather than writing down heroic tales. AHRDO also opened a museum in Kabul: a war museum which was also a peace museum. It commemorated the victims of the various wars in Afghanistan and brought the bereaved together. They were able to exhibit mementoes of family members who had been killed, in what were known as 'memory boxes'. The museum offered a small sense of peace and healing in a deeply wounded country.

When the Taliban took power again in the summer of 2021, AHRDO's work came to an abrupt end. None of those courageous people made it into a German evacuation plane, although many were able to make their way overland to Pakistan and now live in exile in Canada. From there, they continue to document the violence the people of Afghanistan are currently living with. After having to give up their museum in Kabul, they opened a virtual museum, the Afghanistan Memory Home, at the end of 2023 as a tribute to the victims and survivors of decades of armed conflict in Afghanistan.[39]

Working with victims is now a key factor in the concept of transitional justice. Reparations are also part of this: compensating victims is important because it's a material expression of the victims being recognised as such – and the perpetrators are identified. It doesn't always have to be a matter of cash payments. Natascha Zupan reports that in the peace process in Colombia perpetrators had to do community service in affected villages as reparations. The idea is more about acknowledging guilt and a type of symbolic reparation, rather than starkly calculated damages.

Justice or peace? Squaring the circle

Working with victims is crucial for peace processes. However, it often comes up against a very practical problem: in peace negotiations, it's usually the people who waged war who are sitting at the negotiating table. And people with blood on their hands are unlikely to agree to a peace treaty that involves them going to prison for their crimes. Without impunity, war criminals will therefore scarcely agree to a peace treaty – but without justice, and consequently prosecution, there will be no lasting peace.

It isn't a theoretical mind game, but a very real conflict of goals: *peace or justice*? In situations where war rages on, where there's shooting and death, every day sooner that peace is agreed saves lives. In a situation like that, who can – and will – manage to insist on prosecution, reparations and social justice at the negotiating table? On the other hand, a bad peace treaty is already setting the stage for the next conflict. A time after a war is a time before a war, if there is no solid transitional justice – it's squaring the circle, a new problem every peace negotiation has to solve as best it can with a great deal of tact and sensitivity.

Negotiators in processes like this like to refer to the South African Truth and Reconciliation Commission and demand an amnesty for themselves. There was an amnesty clause in South Africa, but it was much more limited than is commonly reported.[40] The basic idea was impunity in exchange for truth, so anyone who made a full confession could apply for amnesty. However, this only applied to politically motivated crimes and had to follow the principle of proportionality. Indiscriminately bombing civilians, for example, wasn't included. Almost ninety per cent of the amnesty requests in South Africa were ultimately rejected. Whether this amnesty clause was a good idea at all is still a matter for critical debate, even to this day. On the one hand, it certainly helped to get a comprehensive picture of the apartheid regime's atrocities, but on the other hand, the victims' rights were pushed into the background and the basic principles of a democratic criminal justice system were suspended.

Natascha Zupan says that in recent times, the issue of transitional justice in peace processes has usually been resolved with the set phrase, 'the most responsible will be held accountable.' How far this can go always depends on the configuration of power at the negotiating table. In this respect, every truth commission and every reconciliation process is always a compromise and can never be perfect. The UN is currently holding talks to determine whether minimum standards for truth commissions and clear criteria for potential amnesties would be a good basis for preventing perpetrators from having an easy get-out clause at the negotiating table in future peace processes.

A strong civil society is key

If nothing else, one insight is clear from the experiences of the last few decades: reconciliation processes must come from ground level. It's essential to have a strong civil society that calls for a confrontation with the past and that is actively involved in coming to terms with it. After the wars in the former Yugoslavian region, for example, there was an initiative for a truth commission, but it failed across the board because the civil society there was too weak and fragmented.

Natascha Zupan cites Spain as an older example. The Spanish Civil War at the end of the 1930s was one of the bloodiest in Europe. General Franco's dictatorship ended in 1975, followed by a shift to democratic elections. According to Zupan, the democratic transition went well. But on a social level, there is still today a deep divide between Francoists and republicans and the war's atrocities are far from being dealt with. The fascists still publicly celebrate the anniversary of Franco's death every year, while over 100,000 victims of the dictatorship still lie buried in unmarked mass graves that are only now slowly being uncovered. Legal investigation of the dictatorship was made more difficult by an amnesty law passed in 1977. Above all, though, there is still a lack of determined effort among civil society to come to terms with the war and the dictatorship.

The Gambia, on the other hand, is a positive example of good civil societal involvement. This small country in West Africa spent 22 years under the dictator Yahya Jammeh's violent rule. It wasn't until 2017 that he had to resign – under massive pressure from the nation's larger neighbour Senegal, even from its military forces. Democratic elections ensued and the new democratic government took several steps towards transitional justice, including drafting a new constitution and establishing a truth commission to investigate the crimes committed under the dictatorship. The commission held public hearings over an incredible 872 days and heard a total of 393 witnesses, all broadcast live on television, radio and YouTube to every corner of the country.

The truth commission ultimately made over 200 recommendations that affected almost every area of public life: from prosecuting perpetrators and/or removing them from the civil service, to changes in the law on freedom of the press and establishing remembrance days and financial compensation for victims. The Gambian government adopted almost every recommendation.[41]

This profound change in The Gambia was made possible by a large number of people taking part in the process. Mobilised by the truth commission's public hearings and with support from international donors, many initiatives emerged at a local level. And as in Kabul, a museum was founded: the Memory House, with the aim of 'making the invisible visible', as the museum's director puts it.[42]

The international community's role in processes that are working to come to terms with the past is controversial. Experts often criticise the fact that external players often ignore a country's or society's actual conditions. And it's true: without precise knowledge of the subtle nuances in these societies and of deeper conflicts, processes initiated externally can completely bypass people. Sustainable reconciliation can only work if confrontation with the past comes from within a society. International actors can help, can finance processes and offer experiences from other post-war societies, but they should always remain supportive rather than be the drivers of a reconciliation process.

Coming to terms takes time

The term 'transitional justice' implies a time limit, a concept of the transition from one form of society to another, or from war to a new peace. There are, in fact, some formal steps that can and must be implemented quickly. But transitions of this kind rarely have a clearly defined ending. Even with exemplary reconciliation processes, it takes time for the deep wounds of the past to have a chance to heal. It takes a long time to rebuild lost trust. And it usually takes many years before a culture of silence can be broken, until a society is even willing to face the atrocities of its own history.

In Germany, too, it took over twenty years. It wasn't until the end of the 1960s that the children of the generation of perpetrators rebelled and asked uncomfortable questions. Until then, there had been continuity at the forefront of politics and the security apparatus, and high-ranking Nazi henchmen were allowed to go on to become judges or even ministers – and this continuity still has an impact today. If we think of the genocide committed by the Germans against the Herero and Nama peoples in Namibia, it took a hundred years for the first tentative attempts to come to terms with the past to become conceivable – and even then, only after great pressure from civil society.

Even though it takes a long time, if the wounds are still open and justice hasn't been established, the next war is inevitable. Transitional justice is a very important building block in defusing conflicts in post-war societies and making a lasting, stable peace possible.

4

LOCAL CONFLICT MANAGEMENT

Even big wars often start small. Feuds between village communities can spark a meltdown if there are deeper underlying divisions, so we should never underestimate them, and we should always look for the wider context behind them. If conflicts can be identified early enough and resolved locally, a meltdown might be prevented.

I experienced this myself in South Sudan, almost in real time. Towards the end of 2010, I travelled to South Sudan in a small group of members of parliament from the Left Party, to get an idea of the situation in the field. South Sudan didn't even exist as an independent country at that time; it was about to secede from Sudan, as a result of a comprehensive peace agreement after a very long, very bloody civil war between the Christian-dominated south and the Muslim, Arab-dominated central government. In July 2011, South Sudan became independent. We went there shortly before that because there was a great fear worldwide that war with the north could break out again while the independence process was under way.

We spoke to many politicians and NGOs in both the north and the south – and came back with another, completely different fear: the threat of war was not so much between north and south, but mainly within South Sudan itself. All the signs were pointing towards turbulence; another civil war was threatening to break out, this time in the new country. All the conflicts and clashes within the south had long been drowned out by the battle in both areas against the hated central government in Khartoum. With the founding of their own state, there was no longer an external enemy who for years had united their own society – a society with an extremely low threshold for resorting to violence after over twenty years of civil war and countless experiences of brute force, and a society in which practically every household had firearms.

Many of the conflicts in South Sudan have local origins and are long-standing, stemming from problems years before the civil war, often between different ethnic groups, frequently involving land, livestock or essential resources such as water, or over power and influence in the community. Traditionally, conflicts like these could be resolved using well-established mechanisms, with the help of village elders, for example. Over the course of the civil war, these mechanisms had been destroyed in many places, or were only a vague memory, replaced by the quick recourse to weapons as a means of supposedly solving problems.

But these traditional conflict resolution mechanisms did once exist – and this is precisely where the concepts behind civil conflict management can step in to revive them and build on them. We heard an example of how this can be effective at ground level from the organisation Nonviolent Peaceforce. It's one of the world's most important organisations when it comes to civil conflict management, and I've had the greatest respect for the work it does ever since that time.

In Western Equatoria, a very poor region of South Sudan, there have long been conflicts between the Mundri, an arable farming group, and the nomadic cattle herders, the Mundari. These conflicts used to be primarily seasonal. After the civil war, they flared up more and more frequently and were fought much more violently. As a result, a small Sudanese organisation turned to Nonviolent Peaceforce for help. Within two months, representatives of the Mundri and the Mundari were sitting around a table. After a long discussion, the two groups came to an agreement and stood together before their communities to promote peaceful coexistence. The mediation was facilitated by African experts who had been trained by Nonviolent Peaceforce.

A very similar story took place in the southernmost area of South Sudan, in the small town of Yei, close to the border with the Democratic Republic of Congo. The organisation Reconcile works in Yei with very similar principles to Nonviolent Peaceforce. The leader, Milcah Lalam, described the dramatic case of two villages where they had just successfully concluded a peace process. For decades, the village communities had lived side by side, as enemies. Again and again there had been mutual attacks, with cattle, children and women being snatched. It was already an unimaginable situation, but then it escalated to extremes. The men of one village attacked the neighbouring village and killed 93 of its women and children. This had never happened before. A vendetta was looming, and with it a never-ending spiral of violence. Faced with this situation, the women from one of the villages asked Reconcile for help. They brought the women of both villages together and managed to reconcile the hostile village communities, over the course of a year – another example of the important role women play in peace processes.

Making peace with a yoga mat

There are so many wonderful examples of how civil conflict management can work at a local level. Well-thought-out concepts lie behind them; concepts developed, propagated and used worldwide by organisations such as Nonviolent Peaceforce and Peace Brigades International. Among specialists, this approach is now referred to as 'civilian peacekeeping', 'unarmed civilian protection' or 'local conflict management'. The principle is based on a simple realisation: there are always conflicts, everywhere. They are unavoidable, and they aren't necessarily a bad thing. In the best-case scenario, they can even be productive. The only thing that matters is working through them without the use of violence.[43]

The concept of civil conflict management is also supported by the German government, which finances two institutions, the Civil Peace Service (CPS) and the Centre for International Peace Operations (ZIF), which train peace workers and deploy them internationally. Although the concept has now reached the corridors of power, it is still often ridiculed there. Unfortunately, there are some people in politics in Berlin who, when calling for civil ways to manage conflicts, are quick to say that you can't persuade Islamic State to make peace with a yoga mat under your arm. They all laugh – and then they go back to discussing weapons. Their goal is achieved, at the expense of a truly valuable tool in building peace. People who can only see conflicts in terms of military warfare see everything else as voodoo or naive.

At its heart, of course, there is some truth in the joke: I wouldn't go to Islamic State (IS) or Vladimir Putin with a yoga mat under my arm either. This cheesy punchline overlooks one thing, though: every conflict is different, and every war or civil war, every escalation of violence, has its own reasons and therefore its own solutions. There isn't *one single* magic formula, *one single* all-encompassing approach to civil conflict management we can use to address all conflicts; there isn't a one-size-fits-all. In the Russia-Ukraine war, a local approach makes no sense at all, but in South Sudan it does. I'm firmly convinced that in – almost – every conflict, there are ways to stop a spiral of violence by civil means. This book is full of examples of how this could work, sometimes on a large scale and sometimes on a smaller one. What these options are, individually, requires very precise analysis of the situation and coordinated measures, if it's really going to work.

An essential feature of civil local conflict management is its preventive character: it's trying to de-escalate a specific conflict in the field and prevent violence from breaking out. If it works, as a rule scarcely anyone notices, because peace isn't newsworthy, unfortunately. During the Covid-19 pandemic, we all learned that 'There is no glory in prevention': successful prevention doesn't lead to fame, because no one notices, no matter how many lives you may have saved as a result. Unfortunately, this also applies to civil conflict management and crisis prevention. 'There is no glory in civilian crisis prevention.'

What do 'civilian' and 'civil' mean?

The concepts behind local conflict management have found their way into government schemes, despite all the yoga mat outrage. However, there's also a certain fraud in the labelling there, and sometimes the word 'civilian' or 'civil' is only added to make military approaches seem more acceptable for the public. For many years, the German government has been pursuing a 'networked' approach to its security policy with civilian and military bodies working together side by side, and foreign military missions, civil conflict management and development aid being closely coordinated. The blurring of the boundary between civilian and military is dangerous, not only for political debate and for developing meaningful conflict solutions, but also in practical terms in the field: if a mediator or a development worker is seen as an extension of an army operation, they lose their credibility and can quickly find themselves the target of armed militias.

There are hugely varying opinions on the question of what 'civil' is and what it isn't. Some people would even include military training, while others would limit the term solely to NGOs. Among pacifists, a very clear definition has become established, and it's also the only sensible one from my point of view: civil means nonviolent. The military is therefore excluded, by its very nature.

From Chicago to the Philippines

As we have seen, exactly what civil conflict management might look like on the ground and which methods might actually work depends very much on the conflict in question, as the following two examples from very different parts of the world will show. They are two encouraging stories that show the great potential of local conflict management. For examples like this, we don't always have to look to the southern hemisphere.

In the US, for example, injury from firearms is the most common cause of death among children and adolescents. In 2023, 17,297 people were shot in the US.[44] In disadvantaged neighbourhoods, gangs have grown in strength and engage in bloody turf wars. Again, with the logic of 'an eye for an eye', every death is avenged and then that is avenged in turn. To break this vicious circle, CeaseFire (now known as Cure Violence) was founded in Chicago a good twenty years ago. It has one simple principle: the people working for it used to be gang leaders themselves, and many of them spent long spells in prison. They come directly from the neighbourhoods where they work. They have street credibility. They are also respected by the toughest gang members, they speak their language, and have a similar history. Their aim is to shift the norms towards ostracism and away from a normalisation of violence. They work using a method of direct intervention: if there's a shooting in their neighbourhood, they're there. They look at who was there, who might now be thinking of revenge, who could break the spiral of violence here and now with an intervention. Their focus is on one goal: to outlaw violence, to reduce deaths. And the statistics prove them right; the National Institute of Justice classifies their work as 'promising'.[45]

The second example comes from Asia. On the island of Mindanao in the south of the Philippines, there have been militant clashes between the Muslim minority and government troops for years, and over a hundred thousand people have lost their lives in the conflict. We've already taken a closer look at the conflict in Mindanao in Chapter 3. Nonviolent Peaceforce (NP) has been active there for years and is accepted and respected by all sides as a neutral force. Despite the 2014 peace agreement, violence in southern Mindanao continues to flare up to this day. NP has observer status in the peace process and has set up an early warning system in various locations on the island so it can react as quickly as possible to local violence.

Early one morning in August 2021, it received news that villagers had discovered around a hundred gunmen heading towards their village. An NP team set out to assess the situation in the field. The root of it was apparently a conflict between two local commanders of the former insurgents, who each controlled individual villages in the area, but who were constantly trying to take over each other's land. It escalated to a shootout on the outskirts of the village, and many civilians were caught in the crossfire. As NP had built up a relationship of trust with all the stakeholders in the region over the years, they were able to get into the thick of the action and ensure the civilian population was safely evacuated. NP then became part of a local ceasefire commission to prevent future escalations in the region.[46]

This is just one of many stories from Mindanao, where NP has played a crucial role in bringing about a peace agreement and ensuring it remains stable ever since it began working there in 2007.

A question of justice

In the last chapter, the example from Poso in Indonesia showed how closely local conflicts on the other side of the world are sometimes linked to our way of life in Europe. The current conflicts there have a lot to do with the car industry's thirst for nickel – and, in turn, with capitalism's thirst for growth and our hunger for cars. It's clear that this is true of many conflicts seen as 'local'. Disputes over land use are often caused by the fact that international corporations have taken over the best land, leaving only pitiful scraps for the local population. Or it might be the lack of rain as a result of climate change, which in turn was largely triggered by rich industrialised countries. In Chapter 12 we'll take a closer look at the causes of conflict and war that originate here in Europe.

In these cases too, anyone who wants to maintain peace must guarantee *justice*. If this doesn't happen, any attempts to deal with local conflicts will merely paper over the cracks and will be doomed to fail. It would be wrong, though, to emphasise a contrast between local and global approaches to resolving conflicts. Both are essential and ideally they can cross-fertilise and complement each other. Local conflict management is a short-term intervention to prevent acute violence. It is important and vital for saving lives practically and quickly and for making a peaceful coexistence possible. It's not a matter of fundamentally preventing conflicts – conflicts are always happening, everywhere, and they aren't the problem. They only become a problem if they aren't dealt with and if they escalate into violence. In this respect, de-escalation is key to local crisis prevention.

At the same time, a solution to local conflicts will only be lasting if the *structural* causes of conflict are eliminated too – including global ones. Fair raw material prices, fair wages, fewer cars and greenhouse gases – fighting for these issues in Europe's corridors of power can be an important contribution to worldwide peace. Of course, I'm not suggesting a violent escalation, but a political one that goes to the root of these conflicts. To be very specific, in Indonesian Poso, it is vital and appropriate that so many people are involved in de-escalating local conflicts. But there will only be a lasting peace in Poso when the nickel mines cease to be a cause of conflict. Here in Europe, we don't share an interest in a peaceful solution in Indonesia: the car industry doesn't share this interest. Its interest is in nickel and it explicitly refers to Indonesia as a 'strategic point'. We have a conflict with the car industry here. To limit its influence, we'd probably have to tackle this conflict head-on here in Europe.

We'll be coming back to nickel later, and not by chance. In Chapter 11, we'll explore the question of why Russia's largest nickel producer isn't being sanctioned. The answer won't surprise you: in this case, too, nickel and the car industry's interests are more important than a peaceful solution.

Prevention starts here

If the causes of war and violent conflicts often lie here with us, it's clear that peace, too, must come from us. Sometimes this can be very specific. We have an absurd situation where the German government finances civilian crisis prevention measures in certain countries while simultaneously approving arms exports to those same countries. Tank weapons for Peru, tanks for Indonesia and tank parts for Egypt have all been approved in the past, while at the same time civil conflict management in these countries was also being funded. This situation hasn't changed under the current government. In December 2023, for example, the German government was forced to admit that it had supported civilian crisis prevention in Pakistan with many millions of euros, and at the same time had approved arms exports to Pakistan amounting to €2.4 million.[47] Supplying weapons on the one hand and believing that the conflicts fuelled by them can be resolved with local peace work on the other is something that simply cannot work. A quite obvious and easy way to manage civil conflicts would be to simply stop exporting weapons to conflict zones.

For local conflict management to have any chance of success, it's essential to have trained experts with knowledge of local conditions – and plenty of them – in all areas with local conflicts. Unfortunately, we found exactly the opposite in Sudan when we visited. There was a German Civil Peace

Service (CPS) employee in a small village in the Nuba Mountains on the border between Sudan and South Sudan. He had been living there for five years and during this time, he had built up a relationship based on trust with the village community – an essential prerequisite for any cooperation. Gradually, through discussions with the village authorities and the various ethnic groups, he was able to help to develop nonviolent concepts of conflict management, resolving problems before they escalated further and became violent – local conflict management at its best.

Unfortunately, he was one of only five (yes, five!) CPS employees in the country – all of whom were also due to be withdrawn, for cost reasons. In a situation where the civil war to come was tangible everywhere, funding those last five peace experts was something the German government considered to be too expensive. This is more or less the complete opposite of a peace-oriented foreign policy.

However, at that time, it wasn't five or even 50 that were needed, but hundreds. At least. And of course, they would all have to be trained first: people from the area, for the area. Building up appropriate training capacities in the more conflict-ridden regions, and in large numbers, is a vital matter of great urgency. Organisations such as NP and many others also provide training as a given, otherwise they wouldn't be able to carry out their work in the various regions they're active in. But it's far from enough. It wasn't enough in Sudan. It didn't take long for a civil war to break out in South Sudan after it became independent in 2011, dragging the already war-torn country even further into the abyss. Could lots and lots of peace workers, in every village and province, have prevented this? I don't know – they might have had a chance. But one thing I do know for sure is that the German soldiers stationed there didn't prevent the war.

As well as local peace experts, it's crucial to have some international stakeholders too, in line with each individual situation. An organisation in South Sudan gave us a very dramatic example of this: in the civil war there, many women were, and are, raped by militiamen when they leave the shelter of their villages to fetch firewood. But not fetching wood is not an option, otherwise they and their families will starve. One solution was simply for women from different countries, and in this context explicitly white women, to accompany the village women. Their mere presence suggested international observation and was enough to deter the militiamen from attacking. Protection through presence: this has for decades and in many countries around the world been the mantra of Peace Brigades International, an organisation that also protects human rights defenders from state violence.

This example shows how one of the factors in effective nonviolent peace work is based on the principle of 'The world is watching'. For politically motivated perpetrators of violence, their reputation throughout the world is crucial: from their point of view, they stand for what is good and right, so they often shy away from committing acts of violence before the public eye worldwide. This is why it is appropriate and important to substantially expand organisations like the German Civil Peace Service, as the Civil Peace Service Forum called for at the beginning of 2023. This forum, an association of many organisations of varying sizes, is politically active and carries out projects of its own. The forum proposed that the Civil Peace Service be expanded from around four hundred to a thousand peace experts in the next few years and that offices for them should also be set up at German embassies.[48]

5

UN PEACEKEEPING FORCES: WHEN TRUST HITS ROCK BOTTOM

'This tragedy will haunt the history of the United Nations forever.'[49] These words were uttered by former UN Secretary-General Kofi Annan. And he was right. He was referring to Srebrenica and to the UN Blue Helmet soldiers who were unable to protect the people entrusted to them. Ultimately, 8,000 people died, most of them boys and men.

The drama began to unfold in 1992. After the collapse of the former Yugoslavia, the Bosnian War broke out: on one side, the aggressors, Bosnian Serbs, supported by the Serbian republic under Slobodan Milošević, and on the other, Muslim Bosniaks, who were hopelessly inferior in military terms. In 1993, the United Nations resolved to establish protection zones for the Bosnian population to prevent 'ethnic cleansing'. One of them was in Srebrenica in the far east of Bosnia, an enclave in the midst of Serb-controlled areas, which would soon become a lethal pressure cooker.

By July 1995, tens of thousands of Bosniaks had fled there. Just 400 UN troops were seconded to protect them. But unfortunately, in that situation, the public eye worldwide was not enough to deter the perpetrators of violence. When the Bosnian Serbs attacked the city in July 1995, there was no defence, and no protection. The totally outnumbered UN forces were not equipped to counter the onslaught and could do nothing but watch as the Serbian troops selected and removed 8,000 Muslim boys and men. They were all later systematically killed: a genocide, as the International War Crimes Tribunal later ruled.

An iconic photo shows the UN commander and the leader of the murderous Serbian troops facing one another, each holding a glass.[50] Many people interpreted it as proof that the UN was collaborating in the genocide, which was wrong, but we'll come back to that later. In any case, Srebrenica was a UN mission that failed so disastrously that it brought practically every UN peacekeeping mission into disrepute – unfairly, in my opinion.

The birth of the peacekeeping force: safeguarding peace

To understand the failure of the UN peacekeeping forces in Srebrenica, we have to go back many years, to 1948, which was when the history of UN peacekeeping missions began, in the Middle East.

With the state of Israel being established on 14 May 1948, there was fierce fighting in the region. The UN Security Council took up the matter and called on all parties involved to agree to an immediate ceasefire. Article 6 of Resolution No. 50 of 29 May 1948 reads literally: the Security Council 'instructs the United Nations Mediator in Palestine ... to supervise the observance of the above provisions, and decides that they shall be provided with a sufficient number of military observers.'[51]

This was the birth of the UN peacekeeping missions, which is still celebrated every 29 May, the International Day of Peacekeepers. Their first mission was entirely unarmed. Although they were military troops in uniform, the Security Council's mandate didn't foresee any armament. Later, this mission was given the name UNTSO: the UN Truce Supervision Organization. Today it still exists under this name, with its headquarters in Jerusalem and led by a Swiss general.

The UN Security Council members probably had no idea of the groundbreaking invention they'd come up with back then. The UN Charter doesn't mention unarmed military operations of this kind *after* a peace agreement or ceasefire. UN military personnel are only provided for in the Charter as a coercive measure against an aggressor who is threatening international peace.

It follows from the logic of war and violence that any kind of agreement requires neutral control. People who are shooting at each other are scarcely likely to trust the people on the other side to stick to any agreements that have been made. We've seen in the previous chapters how ceasefires or peace agreements can come about, but this is always just the first step. The agreements then have to be implemented and honoured, they have to survive minor or major provocations, they have to be immune to misunderstandings, and it's imperative to prevent either side from using a ceasefire to prepare new attacks. This requires people to carry out independent controls and guarantee security – and who would be better suited for this than the United Nations?

Dag Hammarskjöld's three golden principles

Although the next step seems obvious to us from today's perspective, it took a few more years before the United Nations' 'Blue Helmets' became established as an integral part of UN peacekeeping. We have a charismatic UN Secretary-General by the name of Dag Hammarskjöld to thank for this. The Swede surprised the world in the autumn of 1956 with a solution to the Suez Crisis which would, almost overnight, catapult the United Nations from a little-known debating society to a major player in world politics.[52]

The Suez Crisis began with the nationalisation of the Suez Canal by Egyptian President Gamal Abdel Nasser in the summer of 1956. In a coordinated response, Israel, France and Great Britain then attacked Egypt. Israel occupied the

Gaza Strip and the Sinai Peninsula. French and British troops arrived at the canal. All the signs pointed to war – not over oil, as is so often the case in that region, but over a no less valuable resource for the global economy: the fast sea route between Europe and Asia.

The Security Council was paralysed, because two of the aggressors, Great Britain and France, had veto rights over it. As a result, the UN General Assembly took up the matter in its first extraordinary session, and it was Dag Hammarskjöld's hour. In a story that could have come from a thriller, events unfolded at breakneck speed at the General Assembly in the first week of November 1956.

The warring parties were called upon to agree an immediate ceasefire and to retreat. Some countries then pushed for some kind of police to monitor these steps, and the General Assembly called on the General Secretary to come up with a plan. To the entire world's surprise, within a few hours Dag Hammarskjöld presented concrete proposals and principles for deploying a UN peacekeeping force, and the idea was adopted by the UN General Assembly on 5 November 1956 as the United Nations Emergency Force (UNEF-1).

Its task was to monitor the withdrawal of Israeli, French and British troops and then to prevent new escalations, working as a buffer between the Egyptian and Israeli militaries. The troops were armed, but the mandate expressly limited the use of weapons to self-defence only. With the Egyptian government's consent, the UN soldiers made their way along the demarcation line where Israeli territory began; by then the French and British troops had returned home.

And it worked. UNEF-1 was one of the best examples of how much potential there is in UN peacekeeping missions, of how they can stop wars and prevent a huge amount of death, suffering and destruction. It's hard to imagine what would have happened in 1956 if the war machine had carried on and the Nasser government had been overthrown by external forces.

With this mission, the basic rules of the peacekeeping missions were established in practice, and they would later go down in history as the Dag Hammarskjöld principles:[53] first, all parties involved had to agree to UN intervention; second, UN troops had to maintain absolute impartiality; and third, the use of force by the troops had to be limited purely to self-defence.

Srebrenica showed us that these principles were no longer valid. But until the end of the Cold War, they were the golden rules for UN peacekeeping missions. They were only ever deployed *after* a peace agreement or armistice, when there was no more fighting, when there was an agreement and when a neutral authority was needed that both sides could trust. They are colloquially referred to as 'classic peacekeeping missions'.

In the years that followed, the UN Security Council approved many more missions around the globe, from the Dominican Republic to the Congo and from Yemen to Pakistan and India. The ceasefire after the Iran–Iraq war in 1988 was also monitored by a UN peacekeeping mission, UNIIMOG (the UN Iran–Iraq Military Observer Group). In the first two months of their work alone, they received over a thousand complaints – from both sides of the border – about alleged ceasefire violations. All were investigated; most turned out to be trivial. Sometimes, though, shots would be fired or troops would be moved, breaking the agreements. In each case, UNIIMOG was able to ensure the incident was resolved to the satisfaction of both sides.[54] In Europe, too, there's a Blue Helmet mission that has been running for 60 years now and is considered an exemplary classic mission – in Cyprus.

Cyprus: the everyday peace mission

As early as 1964, the UN Security Council approved a peacekeeping force for Cyprus after the conflict between the Turkish Cypriot and Greek Cypriot populations had been steadily intensifying. In 1974, a further escalation ensued with Turkish troops invading northern Cyprus, resulting in the occupation of about a third of the island. After that, a ceasefire was negotiated and a buffer zone stretching 180 kilometres across the island was established between the two regions. Ever since, this buffer zone, or 'Green Line', has been monitored by UN peacekeeping forces.

Since then, the Greek Cypriot section has joined the EU, and the northern part has declared independence as the 'Turkish Republic of Northern Cyprus', although under international law no other country worldwide bar Turkey recognises it. Tens of thousands of Turkish soldiers are still stationed in the north of the island.

The Blue Helmets have been patrolling Cyprus for 60 years, and since there has been practically no military warfare on the island for 50 years you can't help but ask yourself whether this peacekeeping mission still makes sense after such a long time.

One person who answers this question with a resounding 'yes' is Niyazi Kızılyürek.[55] He comes from a Turkish Cypriot family and has been active in the peace movement in Cyprus for many decades. He now sits in the European Parliament, which is a political issue in itself, because the Cyprus that is an EU member is only the southern part of the island, inhabited almost exclusively by Greek Cypriots.

From his point of view, the UN peacekeeping forces have two key roles in Cyprus. The first is continuous de-escalation. There are often minor or major conflicts along the Green Line. Only recently, the Turkish Cypriot side wanted to connect the only mixed village of Pile/Pyla, partly located in the buffer zone, with a road through the neutral Green Zone – which was an absolute no-go for the other side. UN vehicles were unceremoniously pushed aside by construction vehicles, and violence was in the air. Without the peacekeepers as a buffer, the armed forces from the north and south would have met directly at that point. If a shot had been fired in the heat of the moment, a dramatic escalation would have been almost impossible to prevent.

The threat of a potential proxy war on the island is always lurking in the background, too. In recent decades, Turkey and Greece have on more than one occasion been on the brink of a violent conflict – which could have quickly spread to the island. The fact that there have been no military hostilities in the past 50 years is certainly related to the two parties having been gently but firmly kept apart.

The second vital point, according to Niyazi Kızılyürek, is that the Blue Helmets provide very practical reinforcement to the Cypriot peace movement. On both sides of the buffer zone, there are activists who have for decades been advocating reconciliation and reunification. The troops provide essential hands-on support for a variety of activities: conferences, concerts and meetings between the two groups in the Green Line area would scarcely be possible without the day-to-day assistance of UN peacekeepers.

Irrespective of all the positive functions attributed to the UN troops in Cyprus, one thing is absolutely clear: the Blue Helmets do not solve any problems. They won't broker a peace deal between north and south: only the two Cypriot parties themselves can do that. But the peacekeeping force can provide them with the space and time to do so.

Despite all this, the classic Blue Helmet missions are also controversial among pacifists because, ultimately, they are still *military* missions. Military is military, no matter how blue the helmet and how peaceful the intention. As a fundamental stance, I can understand this rejection of the Blue Helmets. But in view of the realpolitik possibilities when it comes to pacifying conflicts, I can take a different stance.

We aren't talking about a perfect world, but about a war that raged in Cyprus. There was shooting, death and expulsion, and it only stopped with the 1974 ceasefire, which was very fragile, at least in its early days. In a situation like that, having a neutrally controlled buffer zone so the hostile armed forces could no longer meet face to face has certainly made the lives of the Cypriot people more peaceful over the past 50 years. That's why I personally think that in individual cases, classic Blue Helmet missions of this kind are important and right – we shouldn't dismiss them.

However, especially in the case of Cyprus, we do need to ask the question of whether the Green Line really needs to be controlled by soldiers. Couldn't civilian 'blue helmets' be used here instead, without any arms? Especially when the conflict has cooled down significantly, if the danger of a proxy war might have been eliminated and there's no longer any need to fear direct military force, I believe that military personnel could be dispensed with.

The end of the Cold War and the advent of the 'robust' missions

All in all, the classic Blue Helmet missions are a truly successful model. However, they're called 'classic' because these days, deployments of this kind are practically never approved.

With the end of the Cold War, they came to an abrupt demise too. From today's perspective, it's hard to understand, but at that time there was a feeling that it was the 'end of history': no more global competition or bloc confrontation, the big problems had been solved and people could now focus on other problems. In the context of war worldwide, that meant civil wars. The battle between the USSR and the US might have been over, but now people felt the world could take care of local conflicts too. The idea was that the UN should play a much greater part in this, as it was no longer the two superpowers' job to corral the smaller ones: the UN, as a whole, could now take over.

There was just one problem. In civil wars, the concept of a peacekeeping force quickly reaches its limits, as the Hammarskjöld principles no longer stand up in civil wars.

How can there be agreement from all sides if one of them is an unofficial rebel group that isn't recognised by the other? How can there be neutrality if only one side has agreed to it? And if the UN forces are no longer neutral and not all the warring parties agree, how can the Blue Helmets act on a non-military basis, or only in self-defence?[56]

Obvious as these questions may seem to us now, back then they were either not asked at all or the answers offered up were disastrous. The UN Security Council members exerted pressure, and the UN Secretary-General at the time, Boutros Boutros-Ghali, delivered the Agenda for Peace, which unfortunately was far from a peace plan. It also explicitly included UN military operations under Chapter VII of the UN Charter, often referred to as 'robust' operations.[57]

Here we need a brief digression into the United Nations Charter, which is divided into chapters. Chapter VI is entitled 'Pacific Settlement of Disputes' – an extraordinarily well-chosen chapter title, in my opinion. It is about diplomacy, negotiations and cooperative approaches to avoiding war and violence. If it should fail, Chapter VII will take effect. It's about 'Action with Respect to Threats to the Peace, Breaches of the Peace'. Here, too, diplomacy is at the forefront; the next step is potential economic sanctions, and if they don't help, Chapter VII makes provision for the use of armed forces 'to maintain or restore international peace and security'.

If things have reached this stage, it's all very far removed from the classic peacekeeping missions. In these circumstances, armed force from the UN is envisaged as a means of ending a war – in other words, UN soldiers on one side to defeat another side by military means, with no neutrality, and no agreement from all sides. This is what's known as a 'robust' mandate, involving a real combat mission and no longer limited to self-defence.

Deployment of UN military forces in this way, as set out in Chapter VII, had never existed before. The concept wasn't new – the Charter was 47 years old at the time – but the reality was new. As a result, the Blue Helmets were no longer purely the 'peacekeepers' they were in Israel, Suez or Cyprus. Now it was all about situations where there was no peace to be preserved.

Almost overnight, a new, very military element was added to the Blue Helmets' operations – and no one was prepared for it, on any level. The UN Security Council wasn't, and neither were the countries sending troops. This became all too clear in Somalia.

At the end of 1992, the United Nations approved a Chapter VII-style military operation for the first time to stabilise Somalia, which had completely collapsed after the fall of the long-term dictator Siad Barre. The culmination of this mission was the battle of Mogadishu, which will be familiar to some people from the Hollywood film *Black Hawk Down*. It is still traumatic for the US to this day, but for the UN, more than anything it was a critical turning point that led to the subsequent disaster in Srebrenica.

The mandates for the UN mission in Somalia constantly changed. It started with an arms embargo, then humanitarian aid was added, and then 500 'classic' peacekeeping troops, before becoming a mandate along the lines of Chapter VII of the UN Charter. The military operation was led by the US, which also provided most of the soldiers. On 3 October 1993, there was a showdown in Mogadishu. The US troops tried to arrest a militia leader in the centre of the city. However, they encountered fierce resistance: three of their Black Hawk combat helicopters were shot down and 18 US soldiers were ultimately killed. It was the greatest loss the US army had suffered in combat since the Vietnam War. The images of a dead American soldier being dragged through the dusty streets of Mogadishu made an impact: the States withdrew all its troops, and the mission was considered a failure.

Crossing the Mogadishu Line

In peace research, this moment is known as the Mogadishu Line – a line that is crossed by becoming a belligerent party in a foreign conflict and consequently having to expect great losses.

I learned this term from Claudia Pfeifer, who researches UN military operations at the Stockholm International Peace Research Institute (SIPRI) in Sweden. SIPRI is one of the most prominent international institutes of its kind, and it has set important standards, especially on arms exports and disarmament. When it comes to the UN peacekeeping missions, there is scarcely another institution that can boast as much experience and expertise as SIPRI.

Claudia Pfeifer impressed me with her explanation of how the failed mission in Mogadishu led to the Srebrenica genocide. When the situation around Srebrenica became more and more precarious, and support was requested from troops at the front line, the commander of the UN troops in Bosnia, General Sir Michael Rose, apparently literally said that the UN in Bosnia would never cross the Mogadishu Line: his troops would under no circumstances fight directly with the Serbian army.[58]

There is so much contained in this statement: the traumatic images from Mogadishu, the dead being dragged through the dust, the US's and the world's shock, and the realisation that a completely different force is necessary for genuine participation in war, for a military fight against an opponent, than is needed to monitor the Green Line in Cyprus. Of course, the statement by the commander on the ground was entirely understandable; not wanting to fight an entire army with 400 Blue Helmets made sense because it was simply impossible. The mistake had already been made much earlier.

The UN Secretary-General had requested a much larger force for the Bosnian mission – he wanted 34,000 soldiers, but the Security Council approved only a fraction of this number.

In the end, just 4,500 soldiers were deployed in Bosnia. No war can be waged, and no one could cross the Mogadishu Line, in a situation like this.

We can see how the UN stumbled into these robust missions completely unprepared. One disaster, Mogadishu, led to the next, in Bosnia. The powers in the Security Council were putting pressure on the UN to intervene in civil wars. But there was a lack of understanding of what participation as a warring party would mean. It was an utterly inconceivable suggestion to first guide tens of thousands of refugees into a 'safe zone' and then to believe that it could be protected by 400 Blue Helmets.

There may have been a psychological element in this. Back then, in the early 1990s, the United Nations was considered sacrosanct. All its military operations had been neutral until then; the UN's troops never took part in the fighting and it held a status comparable to that of the Red Cross: you don't shoot at them. This self-perception persisted, and it gave them a completely false sense of security. The shock was all the greater when the Bosnian Serb troops didn't spare the UN troops but treated them as what they were, by virtue of their mandate: an opposing warring party.

I myself still felt that shock years later. At the beginning of 2003, I joined the UN as a biological weapons inspector. In Baghdad, all the UN facilities were housed in the Canal Hotel. In August 2003, a huge explosion shook the building; a suicide bomber killed 22 people. I was not there at the time myself, but for many years this attack was ever-present in all my UN colleagues' minds, as a warning and a reminder that the days of a neutral UN respected by all sides were over.

Entering into robust mandates and turning away from unconditional impartiality certainly played a crucial role in this. Since then, the risk for UN personnel of becoming a target themselves has increased massively – a development that's probably impossible to reverse now that the UN Blue Helmets' halo of neutrality and inviolability seems irrevocably lost.

Failure all along the line

Mogadishu and Srebrenica were the disasters at the beginning of the robust combat missions. After that, though, it didn't get much better. Today we're in a situation where the UN Blue Helmets have fallen into disrepute worldwide. Not a single new military operation has been approved since 2014, and some of the largest deployments have been, or are about to be, discontinued because the countries concerned no longer want them.

One reason for this is the accusation of a lack of impartiality. In Mali, for example, the UN troops have recently been viewed very critically. MINUSMA, the UN stabilisation mission for Mali, had been operating there since 2013. With around 13,000 soldiers, it was one of the largest UN missions, and also one of the bloodiest: over three hundred MINUSMA members were killed during the last ten years. For a long time, the Blue Helmets were considered a better alternative to the French national military operation – codenamed 'Barkhane' – which pursued purely colonial interests in Mali. Over the years, the boundaries became increasingly blurred and eventually the majority of the population in Mali wanted to get rid of *all* foreign troops. In the summer of 2023, the Malian military government demanded the withdrawal of all UN troops, which is now complete.

As well as partisanship, the UN troops have been accused of many misdemeanours. During an operation in Haiti, they introduced cholera and triggered an epidemic that ultimately killed almost 10,000 people.[59] Mass rapes were proved to have been committed in various operations.[60] Countries contributing troops repeatedly pursue their own self-centred interests when it comes to the missions. Brazil is said to have provided large numbers of soldiers for UN missions for some time in the hopes of getting a seat on the Security Council. Rwanda and Ethiopia are trying to gain political influence by participating in UN missions in the region.

In my view, the concept of robust UN military operations was wrong from the outset. Ultimately, combat missions along the lines of Chapter VII of the UN Charter always entail the UN fighting on one side and trying to win a war by military means. Robust combat missions are the continuation of war by military means to force a decision, and not a peaceful solution – quite a different matter from the classic peacekeeping missions.

The counterargument is, of course, that the world cannot simply stand by and watch genocides like the ones in Srebrenica or Rwanda, where almost a million members of the Tutsi minority were murdered within a few months in 1994. So is there a situation where a bad UN mission is preferable to atrocities like these? The basic idea sounds logical. Only in theory, though; in fact, it falls down because of the reality of the United Nations, which is, first, militarily incapable of real combat missions, and second, structured undemocratically.

Let's start with the second point: the UN certainly cannot be seen as an independent world government that stands above everything and enforces compliance with rules equally from everyone. UN military operations are not agreed by UN headquarters, or by its currently 193 member states. These decisions lie entirely with the UN Security Council, which has five permanent members with veto powers: the US, China, Russia, France and Great Britain. They can assert their own best interests in the Security Council, and that is exactly what they do. When Saudi Arabia violates human rights and bombs Yemen, the Security Council prefers to look the other way, because it doesn't want to jeopardise good relations and trade links. If the Libyan regime violates the same human rights and attacks rebel strongholds in its civil war, there are air strikes and calls for regime change, as relations were already bad anyway. Unfortunately, the whims of these major powers have a great deal of influence in the decisions for or against UN military operations.

Above all, though, the catastrophes of Srebrenica and Rwanda prove that 'a little bit of combat' simply isn't possible. In war, only the principle of 'all or nothing' works. If the UN is to fight on one side in a war, 1,000 or even 10,000 soldiers aren't enough – the UN has to compete with a really large, well-equipped, strong force. And that, in turn, would mean a total militarisation of the United Nations. In my view, the concept of the UN as a military power that could wage war against any country, under the control of a completely undemocratic Security Council, would be horrific.

The future is . . . blue?

The time of robust operations is coming to an end, with good reason. The question remains: what happens next? In view of the success story of the classic Blue Helmet missions, you might think that what's needed is a return to the three Hammarskjöld principles. In fact, what we're seeing right now is a completely different trend.

Military operations are increasingly carried out by regional organisations such as the African Union, while the United Nations is limited to purely political missions, without any soldiers at all. Depending on the situation, the UN takes on civilian administrative tasks, provides humanitarian aid, supports former soldiers with their reintegration or advises on human rights issues – in other words, all the things that are essential in a post-war situation to stabilise a country and make it safer, without military forces or police. Logically, some of the classic peacekeeping missions, such as the one in Cyprus, could also be converted entirely to civilian personnel, as discussed earlier.

These changes in the peacekeeping missions are now also reflected in the UN's strategic planning. In July 2023, the UN Secretary-General published a New Agenda for Peace. The name refers directly to the 1992 Agenda for Peace – and revises it, in at least one place. In 1992, robust missions were explicitly made part of UN policy. The New Agenda clearly states that the Security Council and the General Assembly should 'undertake a reflection on the limits and future of peacekeeping'.[61] It also refers explicitly to the possibility of regional military missions.

Does this trend mean that in the future there will be no Blue Helmets at all? Probably not – a glance at Ukraine is enough to settle that question. Of course, we all hope there will soon be negotiations for peace, or at least a ceasefire. But even this will have to be monitored, as in Israel in 1948 or in Cyprus in 1974. So if there is an amicable solution and both sides agree to it, the three Hammarskjöld principles would be fulfilled and a ceasefire line – however it might be drawn – could be monitored by classic peacekeeping forces. A veto in the Security Council would be extremely unlikely. If Ukraine could reach an agreement with Russia, all five permanent members would certainly be on board.

This in turn would lead to an intriguing problem: Russia has shown that it doesn't adhere to international rules and agreements. Distrust of Moscow is limitless – and with that comes the fear that a soft border monitored by a few unarmed Blue Helmets could simply be overrun whenever it suits the Kremlin. But there could also be a solution to this: if some of the UN soldiers came from countries closely allied with Russia, the border would be fairly secure. China, India, Brazil and South Africa are closely linked to Russia as they are all members of BRICS, a group of leading emerging economies. As mentioned earlier, it's hard to imagine Russia opening fire on Chinese or Indian peacekeepers.

It also wouldn't be the first time in the history of the United Nations that the troops' origin would come into play. In some situations, countries have excluded certain nations from contributing troops, for example in South Sudan, when all Ethiopian Blue Helmets had to leave the country almost overnight due to a border conflict. Such stringent regulation of the forces' nationality couldn't be formally implemented in a Security Council decision, as that would violate the United Nations Charter, which decrees that the provision of troops is voluntary. But of course, this can all be informally ensured in preliminary talks or in peace negotiations.

Whatever a solution for Ukraine might ultimately look like, and whatever role the Blue Helmets might take in it, as long as they are neutral and have consent from all sides, they can always play an important part in peacekeeping until a heated conflict has cooled down to the point where they're no longer needed. The mere fact that the peacekeeping forces exist makes a peaceful solution for Ukraine more conceivable – and therefore more likely.

6

WEAPONS INSPECTIONS

How I was too late to prevent a war, and why it was still the right way

It's not something you do every day. On 5 February 2003, I sat in front of the TV, completely spellbound as I followed a live broadcast from the UN Security Council in New York. It was about war and peace ... and about my own future.

On that day Colin Powell, then US Secretary of State under President George W. Bush, tried to prove in a now legendary presentation that Iraq, under Saddam Hussein, was still running an illegal biological weapons programme. Powell projected slides of mobile weapons laboratories on the wall and even shook some white powder up in a test tube. If it were anthrax, he said, Saddam Hussein could kill all of humanity with it. The only things needed to make this the perfect stage production were fireworks and a fanfare – and the truth.

For it was all a lie. At that time, there wasn't even the slightest hint of a biological weapons programme in Iraq, nor any evidence of it. But the US needed these constructs of lies, as they had serious competition: the United Nations biological weapons inspections. It was a race against time and a battle for the hearts and minds of people all over the world.

Feeling the effects of the 11 September attacks, the United States had already decided to attack Saddam Hussein's Iraq. The biological weapons programme fairy tale was intended to help rally its population, as well as its allies, behind the US government. From mid-2002 onwards, all signs pointed to war, and the fear of biological weapons was stoked worldwide.

This was opposed by a large section of the global community, which wanted to prevent the war at all costs, and which asked a simple question: if there really is evidence that Iraq has a biological weapons programme, why don't we just go and check? The principle of weapons inspections was long established; for Iraq, the UN Security Council had a clear mandate and unrestricted access throughout the country. A peaceful clarification would not have been a problem.

The UN inspectors worked flat out in Iraq to dispel even the slightest suspicion. In a fair world, they would probably have been able to prevent the US offensive. But Washington was determined to avenge 9/11, attacking Iraq in March 2003 and winning the race against time.

Even though they couldn't prevent the war then, weapons inspections can be an extremely powerful tool to resolve escalating conflicts peacefully. Especially in times of war, when every side sets their propaganda machines in motion, fake news can quickly become a justification of war. On more than one occasion, UN weapons inspections have been able to dispel suspicions, helping to avoid a war escalating. They're similar to the Blue Helmets: if they didn't exist, we'd have to invent them.

And what did all this have to do with me? Back then, on 5 February, I was sitting on the suitcases I'd packed to take to Vienna for a three-week training course to become a biological weapons inspector. Whether or not there would be a war also determined whether or not I personally would have to spend three months hunting for bacteria in Iraq. Ultimately, the war happened first, and I wasn't deployed as an inspector in Iraq. Later on, I was involved in analysing all the previous Iraqi inspections at the UN headquarters in New York, which was a fascinating experience too.

Verification: truth or war

How does a biological weapons inspection work? How are you supposed to find illegal bacteria in the middle of a desert? Isn't it an impossible task in a country as huge as Iraq?[62]

It isn't, in fact, impossible, and Iraq is a good example of how the principle of UN inspections works. A quick recap: Iraq did have a very extensive and lethal biological weapons programme. However, that was in the 1980s. It was top secret and only rarely did Western intelligence services see any evidence of it. In 1990, Iraq invaded Kuwait, and in response, a US-led coalition launched a military attack on Iraq. After Iraq's surrender, Saddam Hussein remained in power, but had to agree to extensive UN inspections searching for nuclear, chemical and biological weapons as well as long-range missiles in the country. At first, Iraq denied having a biological weapons programme, but four years later, faced with an overwhelming body of evidence, was forced to acknowledge that it did. After that, under the UN team's supervision, all the facilities were destroyed, blown up, razed to the ground. As a result, Iraq has had no biological weapons programme since 1995. But more on that in a moment.

Inspections are not about investigating a vague suspicion in a country; an inspection's starting point is usually a statement by the country in question. That statement's accuracy is then checked. This is called verification and it's the main approach to weapons inspections, which is why we were called UNMOVIC at the time: UN Monitoring, Verification and Inspection Commission.

Iraq had to make an initial declaration about its biological facilities in 1991. At that point, the Iraqi government was still claiming the facilities were all purely for civilian purposes. This declaration could then be systematically verified: are these facilities really there, are these facilities appropriate for the alleged product, or could something else potentially be manufactured there?

Over the years, Iraq had to keep improving its declarations, which were initially very incomplete, unclear and inconsistent. The Iraqi statements gradually became more and more comprehensive, and their names changed accordingly. Eventually they were 'Full, Final and Complete Disclosures' – in short, FFCDs. When it turned out that they weren't quite full and final after all, there then came – no joke – the 'Currently Accurate, Full and Complete Declaration', CAFCD. In the end, this statement comprised hundreds of pages with every conceivable detail about Iraq's biological activities in the 1980s, including a milk powder factory.

In principle, a country that wants to conceal an illegal programme has two options: either it conceals the secret facilities completely, not mentioning them at all in the declaration that needs to be submitted; or it lists the prohibited facilities, but with a cover story claiming that completely harmless and legal things have been or are still being produced there.

The first option – making no mention of a prohibited facility – seems more obvious. Why should the UN poke its nose in a prohibited production site if it isn't absolutely necessary? But a complete cover-up is almost impossible to maintain. After all, a plant like that wouldn't exist in a vacuum: people work there, things are delivered there, there are invoices and delivery notes and superiors visiting from the ministries. There would be documentation of all these events in an infinite number of places in the country. It is practically impossible to completely isolate that kind of facility without clues to it appearing somewhere else.

If we just consider the scientists who work there, they would have been recorded as working somewhere else previously, and it would be noticeable if they suddenly disappeared. And when an inspection team finds out that at a certain point in the past, a dozen of the country's leading microbiologists have suddenly disappeared and no one knows where they are, it would send alarm bells ringing all the way to the Security Council's meeting room in New York.

Iraq therefore chose the second path. It reported all the illegal biological weapons facilities, but each was accompanied by a pack of lies. The largest and most intriguing plant was 'Al Hakam', where Iraq had produced anthrax bacteria on a large scale in the 1980s, and had sometimes packed them into weapons too. In the statement to the UN, Al Hakam was named, but described as a facility producing single-cell protein for animal feed.

Opening doors instead of throwing bombs

At long last, after training as a weapons inspector, you arrive at a facility of this kind. What's next? A fundamental rule of all inspections is that you must document, photograph and describe everything – absolutely everything, leaving no stone unturned, and as neutrally and objectively as possible, from the outside and inside, recording even the tiniest structural feature. Does it look freshly painted? Can you tell from the floor if walls have been moved? Where do the pipes go? Leaving no stone unturned also means opening every single door, no matter how inconspicuous. You never know what might be behind it: there might be a surprise lying in wait for you.

At the time, I mentioned the UN training course to a journalist friend of mine. Soon after that, she was invited to a factory in Turkey by a German organic clothing manufacturer; following the UN inspection manual, she opened the nearest door on the spur of the moment – only to find a pile of chemical canisters, which would have no place in an organic business.

When the UN inspectors first looked at the Al Hakam plant in 1991, there were question marks straight away. The facility was completely isolated, far from any village. That didn't make much sense for innocent animal feed production. It also had a military design and was closely guarded. Detailed documentation about the facility also showed that although it was in principle suitable for producing single-cell protein for animal feed, the configuration as a whole wasn't optimally designed for that purpose.

So there were inconsistencies, but nothing more. Questions, but no evidence. Iraq remained adamant in its claim that everything produced at Al Hakam was harmless. The next step in clarifying the inspectors' suspicion was taking samples, because nothing is more clear-cut than scientific laboratory evidence of illegal – or at least unreported – bacteria. Of course, when you're taking samples, you have to assume that the accused has done everything imaginable to remove every trace, for example by flushing and disinfecting all the pipes several times. But here, it paid off that the inspection teams were very diverse. They had a wide variety of professional backgrounds and expertise. Some team members had experience of biological production facilities of this kind and knew exactly where even the most scrupulous cleaning has its limits, for example on the seals deep inside the facility. As a result, the plant was dismantled and samples were taken, but they didn't produce a clear result. The fact that the PCR (polymerase chain reaction) method didn't exist in the early 1990s didn't help – today we can use it to detect even the tiniest traces of Covid, but at that time genetic detection was non-existent.

The breakthrough came from taking a completely different approach: the UN team painstakingly compiled a material balance. For every biological production site, whether it produces animal feed or biological weapons, culture media are essential: bacteria are responsible for the actual production in these facilities, and they have to be fed with a culture medium. The UN team collected every shred of evidence worldwide about exports of culture media to Iraq, searched all over the country for invoices and delivery notes – and could ultimately prove that Iraq had imported a far greater quantity of culture media than could be explained by all the production listed in the Iraqi declarations. The discrepancy was so overwhelming that Iraq was forced to disclose its biological weapons programme in 1995. It was a resounding success for the UN inspections.

This result was only possible because UNMOVIC had unrestricted access to all the locations, all the people and all the data. Iraq had to agree to this as a consequence of its crushing defeat in the Gulf War in 1990. This is an important insight for other UN inspections too: the more restricted the mandate, the more difficult the detective work.

From 2004 onwards, I was sitting in the UN headquarters in New York, evaluating the inspections that had gone before. There's one thing I'll never forget: how clear it was in 1995 that Iraq had actually disclosed its entire previous biological weapons programme. I read the transcripts of the interviews carried out with the Iraqis for weeks on end, and it was obvious from everything they said that they were trying to disclose all the details, and to answer all the questions honestly. From 1995 onwards, the UN's biological weapons experts were no longer in any doubt that the programme had been completely laid bare and discontinued.

The doubts were sown elsewhere, for political reasons. In Western capitals, rumours continued to spread that there were still suspicions – for the sole reason that there would still be something to hold over Saddam Hussein. Eight years later, this led to a momentous war, with horrendous consequences for millions of people in Iraq and in the entire region that persist to this day.

This is another lesson learned from the UN inspections in Iraq: they offer the opportunity to investigate the facts independently, but they are not immune from deliberate misinterpretation and political intervention from above.

An alternative to war

In Iraq, the weapons inspection model failed because one side – the United States – was determined to go to war regardless of the outcome. In other situations, though, the model has been a success in every way and has helped to avoid military escalation. Iran is one such example: without the inspections carried out by the International Atomic Energy Agency (IAEA), the nuclear dispute would probably have escalated violently long ago.

It was in 2002 that indications first hinted at Iran's secret nuclear programme. From 2003 onwards, concerted attempts were made to bring about a diplomatic solution; it was a drama of many acts that continues to this day. We will look at it in detail in a later chapter, but for now this will do: in 2012, the nuclear dispute had escalated to such an extent that the entire world was expecting a military strike from Israel on Iran's nuclear facilities. Detailed maps were printed in German newspapers showing the potential flight routes that Israeli fighter jets might take to Iran to bomb uranium enrichment facilities in Natanz or Fordo. However, any further escalation has been averted because Iran agreed to IAEA inspections that went far beyond the normal IAEA routine checks. For example, independent inspectors could check that Iran was complying with agreed uranium enrichment limits. Fears of a potential Iranian nuclear weapon were able to be contained – unfortunately only temporarily, though, because Donald Trump terminated the nuclear accord with Iran in 2018. Since then, only limited inspections have taken place, and the nuclear dispute has once again escalated.

Another example is the Syrian chemical weapons programme. On 21 August 2013, Ghouta, a suburb of Damascus in Syria, was struck by missiles containing the toxic gas sarin. Over a thousand people died in agony; the images shook the world. At the time, Ghouta was in the hands of rebels, so it was suspected that the attack had been carried out by government troops. Within a few days, an agreement was negotiated between the Syrian government, the rebels and the UN to go ahead with an independent inspection. Several hours of ceasefire were agreed for the period between 26 and 29 August 2013, during which the inspectors could carry out their work in Ghouta. Their mission was to determine whether chemical weapons had definitely been used there and if so, which ones.

A former colleague of mine, a doctor at the World Health Organization, was working there. His task was to get the most comprehensive information possible from local doctors about the casualties and their symptoms, as well as laboratory data. He was also able to examine several dozen survivors in hospital himself. They were exhibiting clear symptoms of sarin poisoning, and blood samples also proved beyond doubt that all but two of the 36 patients examined had been poisoned with nerve gases.

Other members of the inspection team took environmental samples at the sites where the missiles, which were allegedly loaded with sarin, had been documented to have hit the ground. They also took samples from the missile remains. Like the medical team, they were able to prove unequivocally that sarin had been used. The UN inspection report to the UN Security Council[63] was an absolutely prime example of how inspections of this kind work, and of the meticulousness with which facts that ultimately provide very clear evidence are compiled.

There was no longer any doubt: sarin had been used in Ghouta. But the inspection team was only allowed to investigate *whether* toxic gas had been used. They weren't able to shed light on the issue of *who* was responsible for it, because that wasn't included in their brief. Still, for the US a 'red line' had been crossed once the use of sarin had been proved. The president at the time, Barack Obama, then approved a military strike against Syria on 31 August 2013, but it didn't actually happen, because in the days that followed, pressure ramped up massively on the Syrian government, even from its close ally Russia. The Assad government finally agreed to stop its entire chemical weapons programme and dismantle it under UN supervision. On 14 September, Syria joined the Chemical Weapons Convention and allowed inspection teams into the country to oversee the complete destruction of all of its chemical weapons and production facilities, and in so doing, a military attack by the US was averted.

These two examples from Iran and Syria show what a valuable tool UN weapons inspections can be for securing peace. They can dispel suspicions or help monitor compliance with agreements as independent witnesses, in a similar way to the Blue Helmets, except that they monitor disarmament agreements rather than ceasefires.

Biological weapons unchecked

The inspections in Syria were carried out by, among others, a team from the Organisation for the Prohibition of Chemical Weapons (OPCW). Its headquarters are in The Hague, and it fulfils the same purpose with chemical weapons as the IAEA does with nuclear weapons: both bodies implement and monitor UN treaties prohibiting certain weapons.

The OPCW's daily functions are twofold. First, it monitors all chemical factories worldwide that claim not to produce prohibited chemical weapons, but would be able to do so, due to their configuration; and it carries out standard verifications – the information provided by the operating companies is checked to ensure that production really is exclusively for peaceful purposes and that there's no improper use for military purposes.

The other task used to be gargantuan, but is hardly ever called for any more: the task of destroying existing chemical weapons in the member countries. The ban on chemical weapons only came into force in 1997. At that time, the US and Russia in particular still had huge quantities of deadly chemicals, bombs and missile heads that had to be destroyed systematically and, above all, safely. In these countries, and later in Syria, the OPCW monitored the destruction of every chemical weapon, and of the facilities producing them.

While there are large organisations with permanent inspection teams for nuclear and chemical weapons, there's no such body presiding over biological weapons. What's the difference between biological and chemical weapons? A biological weapon is one that uses living organisms to harm an enemy's people, animals or plants. They are usually pathogens such as viruses or bacteria which are used to trigger epidemics. Chemical weapons, on the other hand, use highly toxic chemicals, usually lethal even in the smallest quantities, such as chlorine gas, mustard gas or the nerve agent sarin.

There has been a comprehensive ban on biological weapons since 1975 – but without any provision for monitoring it. After the end of the Cold War and agreement to the extremely comprehensive chemical weapons ban in the 1990s, this gaping omission should have been plugged. What was known as a verification protocol for biological weapons was drafted over many years, but was ultimately never implemented. In 2001, negotiations broke down under resistance from the US, which considered the secrecy of its own laboratories and industries more important than worldwide monitoring of the ban on biological weapons – a fatal error.

This means that to this day, there are no worldwide routine UN biological weapons inspections. The inspections in Iraq mentioned earlier were based on special UN Security Council mandates that related exclusively to Iraq. A permanent inspectorate, like the IAEA for nuclear weapons or the OPCW for chemical weapons, does not exist for biological weapons, even now.

If there are biological weapons allegations against a country, the only opportunity for an international investigation lies with the UN Secretary-General, who has the mandate to demand a UN inspection if in doubt. Among experts, this is known as UNSGM, the 'UN Secretary General's Mechanism'.[64]

This mechanism was established in 1980 by a UN General Assembly resolution and was originally intended for investigations of both chemical and biological weapons; the OPCW was founded later. However, there are no established bodies for this, nor any permanently employed, trained inspection teams. In case of doubt, the Secretary-General would have to ask member countries or other UN organisations to provide the appropriate staff.

Never believe it but always take it seriously

In my view, this is an untenable situation: inspections are crucial for de-escalating conflicts. They are also indispensable for dispelling unjustified accusations. In virtually every conflict, at least one of the sides accuses the other of using, or having used, biological or chemical weapons. It's precisely because they're banned and internationally ostracised, and precisely because they're so horrific, that they're the perfect fodder for propaganda against the enemy. Very often, accusations like this are simply nothing but propaganda – but sometimes they aren't.

This is why my own basic rule in dealing with this kind of accusation is as follows: never believe it, but always take it seriously, and always investigate it. It could be fatal to ignore even one single story about the alleged use of chemical weapons or to dismiss it as propaganda: if it turned out not to be propaganda, if a toxic gas had been used, the perpetrators would simply get away with it scot-free, and could feel emboldened to carry on.

This isn't purely theory: it has happened, at least once, with appalling consequences. The backdrop was once again Iraq. At the end of the 1980s, Saddam Hussein waged a war of annihilation against the Kurdish population in the north of the country. For over a year, he repeatedly used chemical weapons in the 'Anfal campaign'. The world looked away, even though there were enough clues for alarm bells to ring. Kurdish organisations had repeatedly made claims about the chemical attacks internationally. At that time, though, Saddam Hussein was still being courted by the West. He was a welcome ally in the fight against Iran, so no one was interested in the chemical weapons he was using – well, no one except the European companies that supplied him with the chemical facilities and the appropriate missiles.

Then came 16 March 1988, a date still deeply etched into the Kurdish people's collective memory. The Iraqi air force bombed the city of Halabja with chemical weapons; over five thousand people died, and images of dead children in the city's streets spread around the world. I have visited the mass graves in Halabja, and all the time I was there, only one thing went through my mind: they could all have been saved. They would all still be alive if the world had taken the reports of Saddam's chemical attacks seriously, if it had intervened sooner. That's why this basic principle is so important: always take it seriously, always investigate it. And this is why we need the United Nations weapons inspections.

Of course, there's also the option of civil organisations investigating this kind of suspicion, either because the UN refuses to investigate for political reasons – which can quickly become the case in view of the UN Security Council's veto powers – or to substantiate initial suspicions to the extent that the international community takes up the matter. In 2023, I was in northern Iraq with a colleague from International Physicians for the Prevention of Nuclear War (IPPNW) to investigate suspicions that the Turkish army was using chemical weapons against the PKK (the Kurdistan Workers' Party) in its operations in northern Iraq.[65]

The problem with civil investigations, though, begins with access. The Kurdish autonomous government in northern Iraq, which works closely with Turkey, had sealed off the combat zones in the north. A local organisation had documented the case of a farmer who claimed to have been attacked by Turkish soldiers with chemical weapons. The doctors treating him at the nearby hospital had also initially determined that chemicals might have been involved. Later, under pressure from the Kurdish autonomous government, they had to revise their statements. In our civil reconnaissance mission, we weren't even able to visit the hospital in question or the farmer's village to at least gather first-hand reports. And because we couldn't even get close to the crime scene, the plan to take samples on site and have them examined in independent laboratories also had to be shelved.

From many conversations with local organisations and from watching stacks of footage, we were able to formulate an initial suspicion – which in our view should have been sufficient for an international investigation – but nothing more. Without unhindered access to all the locations, facts and people, there's no chance of irrefutable evidence, for example in the form of samples that could be examined in an independent laboratory.

On the other hand, there are examples of civil inspections that have been very effective. In the next chapter, for instance, we'll take a closer look at the investigation of an anthrax outbreak in the Soviet city of Sverdlovsk (now Yekaterinburg). That investigation was one of the few successful civil biological weapons inspections that I'm aware of. It didn't prevent war or change the course of history, but it did show one thing: with perseverance and good scientific research, even the smallest, most clandestine bacteria can be detected. No one should be under the illusion that illegal weapons programmes can be kept secret from inspectors in the long run.

Of course, it's also because of my personal history and my time at the UN that I hold UN weapons inspections in particular in such high esteem. But the verification of Iran's nuclear programme or the destruction of Syria's chemical weapons facilities are glowing examples of how dangerous crises can be defused by peaceful means, even if you ignore my own enthusiasm. I don't even want to imagine what the world would look like today if there had been air strikes on Iran or Syria back then. That's why the gaping omission when it comes to biological weapons is so worrying.

This is also where a peaceful foreign policy could start, as the only thing fundamentally missing is money: even without a formal verification protocol, interested countries can of course set up a permanent inspectorate at any time, train up suitable experts from all over the world, certify laboratories and keep the necessary equipment in stock. With the UN Secretary-General's mechanism (UNSGM) mentioned earlier, there is a mandate for biological weapons inspections too. It could be used much more effectively in years to come if the Secretary-General also had the appropriate resources at their disposal.

7

Using science against war propaganda

Have you heard of Mr **S**chrader, Mr **A**mbros, Mr **R**itter and Mr von der Li**n**de? They were four chemists who researched increasingly lethal nerve gases during the Nazi era and ultimately invented sarin. They were so proud of their invention that they concocted the word 'sarin' from their own surnames, crowing about having created one of the deadliest weapons in the world.

This wasn't an isolated case: the history of science is also a history of war. It's often been unwitting and unintentional, as it was with Robert Koch's discoveries about bacteria, which formed the basis for the biological weapons attacks in the First World War, or with Albert Einstein's work, which paved the way for the atomic bomb. Almost every technical innovation has been used for military purposes: satellites, lasers, drones – the list is endless.

However, it would be a mistake to consider the sciences to be solely on the war machine's side and driving the constant development of new weapons, as they can also play an important part in peace work. They can help us uncover war crimes, verify disarmament agreements or expose war propaganda. How this can happen and the enormous but dormant potential for a more peaceful world can be illustrated with the example of a very special man: Matthew Meselson.

You might have heard of him from your biology lessons: in 1954, he used a great experiment to demonstrate how DNA duplicates itself when cells divide.⁶⁶ It brought him considerable scientific fame, which he was able to exploit to the full to promote his political work in favour of disarmament and arms control. In fact, he's probably one of the very few people who can claim to have brought about the abolition of an entire class of weapons of mass destruction. Many years ago, he told me how it came about during a long conversation in his modest office at Harvard University in Cambridge, Massachusetts.

Biological weapons are too cheap – they should be banned

In the early 1960s, the newly elected US President John F. Kennedy founded an arms control bureau. The Arms Control and Disarmament Agency (ACDA) was tasked with developing alternatives to the nuclear arms race and submitting disarmament proposals to the president. Well funded by Kennedy as a political project, ACDA faced a problem well known to many public bodies at the end of their first year: money has to be spent before the end of the year to avoid budget cuts the next.

ACDA made a virtue of necessity and invited renowned scientists from all over the US to spend several months on a research residency. Meselson hastily agreed, although he had scarcely had any dealings with disarmament issues. He was interested from a political point of view, though, influenced by his doctoral supervisor Linus Pauling, a Nobel laureate in chemistry who had campaigned fiercely against atomic bomb tests and who is widely considered to have fathered the first, limited test ban treaty. Pauling was deeply convinced that science *must* intervene in political and social issues.

Meselson's stay at ACDA gave him access to some highly classified information: anyone meant to be developing disarmament ideas for the US government first needs to know what its armed forces are researching. And so it came about that after an extensive security check, he was granted access to the inner sanctum of the American biological weapons programme in Fort Detrick, Maryland.

Since the end of the Second World War, biological weapons of all kinds for use on humans, animals and plants had been developed there. Anthrax, plague, rabbit fever, botulinum toxin as well as rice and wheat diseases were produced in huge quantities and stored in the event of war. It was a horrific arsenal. Biological weapons require extensive research and development, and the effective propagation of viruses and bacteria is far from simple. Compared to nuclear weapons, though, the expense involved is considerably less. Meselson asked what the point of it all was – and was given the equally plausible and banal reply that biological weapons are simply much cheaper than any other weapon of mass destruction.

Meselson was still a newcomer to biological weapons at the time, and maybe that was why he had the necessary distance to intuitively recognise that this was also an argument *against* an American biological weapons programme. If they're that simple and cheap, other countries could follow the American example, thereby undermining the US's military supremacy – simply and cheaply.

In 1963, only a handful of nations had atomic bombs, and nuclear technology was very complex and expensive. Meselson sensed that the strategic advantage for the US as a world power lay not in cheap weapons but in the ones that were too expensive and difficult for potential adversaries to produce. These weren't moral considerations. Back then, it was purely a power-related argument that Meselson was formulating. It followed a logic that was as patriotic as it was military – and so it was perfect for an inveterate power-driven politician such as Richard Nixon, who would go on to become president of the United States in 1969.

In the 1960s, Meselson worked in Harvard University's Biological Laboratory. He usually took his lunch at the cafeteria in an institute nearby, where he regularly met with another Harvard professor: Henry Kissinger. In spite of their differences, a close friendship developed between the two of them. Kissinger was a Republican, while Meselson went to Washington to assist the Democratic presidents Kennedy and Johnson. However, they were united by a common interest in international politics and the arms race between East and West, which was raging unchecked at the time.

Until 1969, Meselson acted as Kissinger's eyes and ears in Washington, regularly reporting back to him on the latest developments in the White House. With Nixon's election as president, they would swap roles. When Henry Kissinger became National Security Advisor he relied completely on his old friend and colleague from Harvard when issues relating to biological weapons arose. 'What shall we do about your thing?' he asked Meselson at the very beginning of his term in office. Meselson saw his chance and took it.

In the weeks that followed, he wrote several memoranda on the dangers of biological and chemical weapons in which he repeatedly addressed the one question that had been on his mind since 1963: why should the US, as a world power with a huge nuclear arsenal at its disposal, show the world how to make a simpler and cheaper weapon of mass destruction?

It's difficult now to say with certainty which factors drove Nixon to ultimately abandon and destroy the US's enormous arsenal of bioweapons. Meselson says he isn't sure what role he played in it himself. But he is quite sure that it was the argument about biological weapons being *too* cheap and *too* simple that finally tipped the scales. On 25 November 1969, Richard Nixon announced that the United States would destroy its entire biological weapons arsenal and would only conduct biological research for peaceful and defence purposes from then on. This cleared the way for negotiations on a global ban on biological weapons. Three years later, the international Biological

Weapons Convention was signed in Geneva, prohibiting any development, production or stockpiling of biological weapons worldwide – a fabulous result.

The end of Agent Orange

Several years earlier, Meselson had already been attracting attention as a peace activist. US soldiers had been deployed in the Vietnam War since 1965. The weapons used included huge amounts of tear gas and the notorious Agent Orange. Even though they weren't toxic nerve agents, their use was scarcely any less deadly. Tear gas was mainly used to force enemy fighters out of hiding and then shoot them. And the plant toxin Agent Orange contained so much dioxin that even today it still has dramatic consequences for the inhabitants' health in the areas affected by it.

Matthew Meselson saw the threat of chemical escalation in the battlefields of Vietnam and took action. In the course of 1966, he managed to mobilise over five thousand scientists in the US, including 17 Nobel Prize winners.[67] Using a petition, they called on President Johnson to bring an immediate halt to the use of all chemical weapons against people and plants in the Vietnam War. They pointed out that the use of any chemical weapon can quickly lead to other, even more lethal toxins coming into play, making a chemical escalation inevitable. Above all, though, Meselson took up his old argument in the petition that when it came to chemical and biological weapons, many countries could quickly acquire weapons of mass destruction. This could only be prevented by a comprehensive ban: 'The barriers to the use of these weapons must not be allowed to break down.'[68]

Nevertheless, the combined power of science achieved scarcely anything. By the end of 1969, more than six thousand tonnes of tear gas had been sprayed in Vietnam, and the use of Agent Orange continued unchecked. Resistance to the Vietnam War was becoming increasingly radicalised, barricades were burning down worldwide, and the police were using tear gas tested in Vietnam to counter demonstrations. But Meselson carried on his work as usual behind the scenes in Washington and within the scientific community. He was soon considered the leading critic of chemical and biological weapons in the US. In 1969, he was eventually commissioned by one of the most well-known scientific organisations in the world, the American Association for the Advancement of Science (AAAS), to investigate the ecological consequences of Agent Orange and other plant toxins in Vietnam. With a budget of $50,000, he flew to Vietnam with a small team for six weeks in August 1970.

The plant toxins that were sprayed in Vietnam are often trivialised as defoliants. This isn't untrue: they were also used to kill off large areas of trees in the Vietnamese jungle to give a clear view of the enemy Viet Cong guerrilla fighters' potential hiding places or supply routes. To this day, though, it's largely kept quiet that the poisons were mainly used to destroy rice paddies. Without rice, there would be no Viet Cong, according to the Americans' logic.

So the area Meselson would investigate consisted mainly of paddy fields. Against all odds, he and his team managed to organise a helicopter for their mission on the ground. They were asked by a local commander to investigate the results of a spraying operation along the Sông Re river in the province of Quang Ngai. The armed forces stressed that this area could not possibly be rice fields for the local population. There were no houses, huts or any other sign of settlement in the area, they said, and the rice paddies had only just been created. According to the army, this was a clear sign that the rice fields belonged to the Viet Cong guerrillas.

What Meselson saw and documented in the coming days was to make a decisive contribution to President Nixon's complete abandonment of the use of plant toxins in the war a few months later. The entire valley was clinically dead; all the trees and plants were leafless and withering. And, of course, the area around the river was inhabited – by the Montagnard, an ethnic minority in Vietnam. Even on the American maps, every single one of their houses was precisely recorded. Meselson photographed them all from the helicopter. The rice terraces had been there for decades (and would later even be found on French maps dating from 1938). Meselson's team contacted the Montagnard and interviewed the residents. The data proved that it wasn't the Viet Cong's food source that was destroyed in the paddy fields but a local village population's.

Meselson documented everything with meticulous precision. To this day, his photos from August 1970 are gruesome documents of a habitat's total destruction. Back in Saigon, he presented all the results to the commander-in-chief of the troops in Vietnam, who candidly admitted to him that the use of plant toxins had no real military benefit. The defoliation of jungle areas didn't make much sense, because it took the leaves weeks to fall off after they had been sprayed. By then, the area of operations had usually shifted.[69]

Meselson's team's data was impressive enough to convince both the American ambassador in Saigon and the military commander-in-chief on the ground. In a joint statement, both spoke out in favour of an end to the use of poisons. In the military establishment, though, this request met with fierce resistance; and at first, nothing happened in Washington. It was only when a reporter from the *Washington Post* got hold of the statement from the two eminent figures in Saigon that the White House reacted. On 26 December 1970, the day before Meselson presented his research findings at an AAAS meeting in Chicago, Nixon declared a halt to all plant toxin use in Vietnam. Three years later, in 1973, Nixon finally withdrew US troops from the deadly war in Vietnam.

Yellow rain over Asia

A few years later, Meselson once again took on the establishment. The story began at the end of the 1970s, after the

Vietnam War was over. Members of the Hmong tribe in Laos told of attacks by Vietnamese and Laotian forces, describing a yellowish, pathogenic precipitation that became known as 'Yellow Rain'. In the West, suspicions arose that the Soviet Union was providing support to its communist allies in Laos and Vietnam by supplying them with chemical weapons. This seemed to be confirmed in July 1981 when an American laboratory detected potent fungal toxins – a typical biological weapon – in the yellow particles.

The US government was convinced it was a chemical weapons attack. US Secretary of State Alexander Haig claimed in autumn 1981, 'We have now found physical evidence from Southeast Asia which has been analyzed and found to contain abnormally high levels of three potent mycotoxins—poisonous substances not indigenous to the region and which are highly toxic to man and animals.'[70] At first, Meselson had no reason to doubt this official version. Nothing changed until a good year later, when a British scientist came up with the idea of placing the particles under the microscope. To his astonishment, what he found was primarily pollen. It was all rather unusual for a chemical weapon.

The US government went on the offensive. In November 1982, it held a press conference to announce that Yellow Rain was a mixture of fungal toxins, solvents and pollen. Pollen was seen as an optimal carrier for the poison, as it is easily inhaled and remains in the lungs, where the toxin can do its lethal work. The particularly treacherous thing about it was that the pollen would guarantee the weapon a long-term effect. Even if the precipitation settled, the pollen would be stirred up afresh with every little gust of wind, posing a new threat.

Meselson was perplexed. He'd seen the yellow particles with his own eyes. They were compact specks almost the size of grains of salt; wind wouldn't have been able to stir them up. There was clearly something wrong with the chemical weapons hypothesis. Meselson was intrigued enough to embark on a scientific expedition that would take him into completely unknown territory.

He obtained samples of Yellow Rain from various sources and invited some colleagues from different disciplines to a meeting at Harvard to discuss potential explanations. No one there had ever heard of yellow precipitation or small clumps of pollen containing fungal toxins before. A botanist established that the pollen in the particles all came from Southeast Asian plants that are fertilised by bees. Straight away, they called Professor Thomas Seely from Yale University, who had been studying Asian bee species for years and was considered a worldwide authority on them. They told him about the Yellow Rain and the government's chemical weapons theory. After a long pause, Seely began to laugh and uttered just one sentence: 'That is bee shit.'

Bees are careful not to soil their own nests. They only relieve themselves in the open air, while they are flying, a phenomenon known as a 'cleansing flight'. After being fed as larvae in the hive for weeks on end, the newly hatched bees have to get rid of a large amount of accumulated faeces on the first flight they make in spring. When they swarm in large numbers at this time, the phenomenon of yellowish rain occurs.

The bee shit theory seemed a bit odd at first, but it was the only feasible explanation for the phenomenon to date. Meselson set out to scientifically substantiate the theory. The crucial question was whether the pollen in the yellow rain was actually eaten by bees in the area. The answer was on his doorstep. Harvard University has a museum where generations of researchers have collected a multitude of objects from all over the world. Pinned up in an exhibit on the top floor were three dried specimens of the bee species that lived in the area they were investigating – and that fed on pollen.

As it was a matter of national security, Meselson took a specimen of each species to his laboratory, carefully rehydrated them and then crushed them, using scientific methods.

Decades-old bee droppings emerged from one end. It's important to note here that pollen grain shells are some of the hardest and most resilient things produced in nature. Even if every other element of the pollen has long since decomposed, the shells will last for hundreds or even thousands of years. It's also possible to definitively determine which plant species the pollen originated from by the shell's outer shape.

It turned out that Meselson's samples contained exactly the same types of pollen that had been found in the Yellow Rain, which seemed to prove that the insidious aggressors in the Asian jungle weren't in fact Soviet chemical weapons engineers, but simply bees. But Washington continued to defend itself vehemently, claiming that because there were no long winters in the tropics, and it was always the same temperature, there was no reason for cleansing flights. And if Meselson's theory were correct, the phenomenon of Yellow Rain would have to occur all over Asia, but at that point it hadn't been documented anywhere.

Only a bee research expedition to Asia could provide the ultimate proof. The American MacArthur Foundation contributed $5,000, and Meselson set off with Seely. In Bangkok, a Thai bee specialist joined the team. Seely knew the locations of some bees' nests in the area near the Laotian border from earlier research trips. When they got there and found the nests, they laid out large sheets of white paper around the trees where the bees were nesting, in the hope of catching droppings. Just a few hours later, they were completely covered with lots of small yellow deposits. As they carried on with the expedition, they were even able to directly observe Yellow Rain occurring twice. Back in the US, Meselson and Seely published their results, and the biological weapons theory was clearly refuted.

Anthrax over Sverdlovsk

Around the same time, Matthew Meselson was also involved in another alleged bioweapons case. In 1979, reports reached the West from the Soviet city of Sverdlovsk (now Yekaterinburg) that dozens of residents there had died of anthrax poisoning within the space of a few weeks. In the West, there was already a suspicion that a Soviet military facility in Sverdlovsk was working on biological weapons. The obvious conclusion was that the anthrax bacteria had entered the environment from there. The Soviet leadership, though, explained that animals in the area around Sverdlovsk had contracted anthrax naturally and that several people had become ill from eating meat infected with it – a perfectly plausible explanation, since undercooked meat contaminated with anthrax does lead to anthrax outbreaks worldwide.

In March 1980, Meselson was invited to the CIA's headquarters in Langley, Virginia to evaluate the data that was available. From what he could see, there were essentially two pieces of information that contradicted each other. On the one hand, the illnesses in Sverdlovsk dragged on for two months, which pointed to an infection through contaminated meat. On the other hand, the CIA had an informant in the city who was quite sure that it was pulmonary anthrax, not gastrointestinal anthrax – in other words airborne infection, which in turn suggested a potential accident in an anthrax factory. Only an independent on-site inspection could provide clarification, but of course that was unthinkable given the political conditions in the early 1980s.

It was not until the downfall of the Soviet Union that Meselson was given the green light for a mission at ground level: a mission that was to be an unexpected success. With a small research team, Meselson managed to prove that in 1979, a cloud of the deadly bacteria had in fact passed over Sverdlovsk, and had originated from a secret military compound in the heart of the city. The investigation's starting point was a list of all the 1979 fatalities, including their precise addresses. This gave the team's sociologist, Meselson's wife Jeanne Guillemin, the opportunity to determine each victim's exact whereabouts at the time. She and an interpreter spent weeks working their way through all the victims' relatives and acquaintances. The results of their labour are fascinating. While the anthrax victims' homes were indiscriminately scattered across the city, their whereabouts during the day were concentrated in a narrowly defined corridor southeast of the secret military compound. On the map, it was literally possible to see a deadly cloud dispersing towards the southeast like a plume of smoke.

The proponents of the meat theory were essentially relying on several documented cases of anthrax in animals that had occurred near Sverdlovsk in the spring of 1979. However, the team was able to show that without exception, all of these animal anthrax cases had occurred in villages located in precisely the same very narrow corridor southeast of Sverdlovsk identified by Guillemin on the basis of the anthrax victims' locations.

Today, there is no longer any doubt that highly infectious anthrax bacteria were released from a military facility in Sverdlovsk in 1979. How exactly it could have happened is still unclear, though. There is a much cited but unproven hypothesis that anthrax spores were processed on a large scale there. All of the air extracted from the secret facility would have had to be cleaned with fine dust filters to prevent bacteria escaping. When a filter was being replaced, it is possible that a mistake occurred and went unnoticed for several hours. During this time, an anthrax cloud could have escaped and drifted over the city, with the wind, towards the countryside. Whatever the exact cause, it was a triumph of science to be able to provide clear evidence of a biological weapons accident 13 years after the event – an excellent scientific thriller, which Jeanne Guillemin has published in all its details in a gripping book.[71]

Science and peace research

Matthew Meselson is certainly an exceptional personality. He has achieved almost everything in his scientific career, from the most elegant experiment in the history of biology to the Lasker Award, the US's highest accolade in medical science. Above all, though, his story can teach us that a critical mind, well-researched facts and scientific evidence are the best means to fight war propaganda and to campaign for strong arms control. It's just a matter of getting down to it – and unfortunately that's still the problem today across the world.

Although there are professorships for scientific peace research at some universities, and individual scientists have come together in an informal network to research the subject, this is a very narrow niche, in both senses: there are scarcely any scientists in peace research; and in the sciences there are practically no references to war, peace or disarmament in research and teaching. One possible exception here is physics, which was profoundly rocked by the development of the atomic bomb and is still the most likely to look at the issue of scientific responsibility. In my studies as a biologist, I never came into contact with this kind of issue; as students, we had to take the initiative ourselves to raise questions about, for example, the risks of genetic engineering.

Now is the time to establish a much stronger link between science, technology and peace work. In the sciences, there needs to be a much stronger emphasis on critical reflection on potential military abuse of scientific achievements. This could function as a kind of early warning system to foresee military uses and to promptly initiate potential disarmament negotiations; we'll look into this in more detail later, in Chapter 13. When it comes to disarmament and arms control, we need plenty of Meselsons who can use their scientific skills to review treaties, to develop measuring processes and to verify claims in the field so that fake news and war propaganda can be refuted through reliable facts.

8

NEWS MAKES WAR

Like the second Iraqi war, the first one began with a lie too. And what a huge lie it was! In August 1990, Iraq invaded and annexed the small neighbouring country of Kuwait. On 10 October 1990, a US Congress committee organised a hearing on the Iraqi invasion of Kuwait. In tears and clearly shaken to the core, a young Kuwaiti nurse described the inconceivable brutality of the Iraqi soldiers in Kuwait: she said they had stormed into her hospital, taken the premature babies out of their incubators and left them to die on the cold floor.

The president at the time, George H.W. Bush, repeated this story over and over; the American people were convinced, and the vicious demon Saddam Hussein had to be stopped. Three months later, an international coalition led by the US launched attacks on Iraq.

Iraq's invasion of Kuwait was real; it was contrary to international law and it had to be condemned. But everything else about this story was bogus and a lie. Not a single baby had been taken from an incubator, the nurse was not a nurse, the committee was not a committee at all, and everything had been staged by a close confidant of George Bush. A year later, the *New York Times* uncovered the story behind the story, which has since found its way into the hall of fake news with the title 'the incubator lie'.[72]

The lie was orchestrated by a man named Craig Fuller, Bush's former chief of staff and the most influential man at Hill & Knowlton, the US's largest PR agency at the time.

Financed by the Kuwaiti government in exile to the tune of over $10 million, the mission was to galvanise public opinion in the US in favour of a war against Saddam. The whole country was convinced by a widespread wave of propaganda, but the dead babies were at the heart of the action: dead babies always do the trick.

Some well-meaning members of the US Congress were drummed together for this purpose and organised into an informal 'human rights caucus'. This caucus set up the hearing on the Iraqi invasion as a completely informal event – which was important, because it meant that the witnesses weren't questioned under oath and could lie until they were blue in the face without any comeback. The alleged nurse was the daughter of the Kuwaiti ambassador to the US, meticulously prepared for her performance by the PR agency. An excellent 1992 report by the German broadcaster WDR documents a visit to the Kuwaiti hospital in question. The manager being interviewed is very clear in her statement that babies were never taken out of incubators there.[73]

Truth: always the first victim of war

Fake news isn't an invention of the internet age. People have been lying for centuries – especially when it comes to war. Or before the war, when it's a matter of closing ranks and morally legitimising the bloodshed to come. When we read treatises on fake news today, one thing stands out: it's always associated with extremists, criminals or dictators. The incubator lie and Colin Powell's anthrax performance before the UN Security Council in February 2003 show that democracies resort to targeted disinformation too, when it comes to war and peace.

This leads to a very sober realisation: critical journalism is also peace work. Unfortunately, the work of the *New York Times* and WDR came too late; they were only able to expose the infamous incubator lie months later, by which time the war was almost over. However, the potential – and necessity – of an independent media industry becomes plain to see: if ruling powers have to worry about their war propaganda being exposed, their boundaries are set for them: boundaries that have to be drawn afresh every day by exposing propaganda lies, debunking half-truths and critically questioning every story. It's a requirement that unfortunately clashes far too often with the reality of time constraints and the work that goes on in the world's editorial offices.

War lies aren't always as dramatic as the incubator narrative. Sometimes a ruler's manipulations are much more subtle and scarcely identifiable at first glance, even by the most critical media. Or mistakes simply creep into reports: mistakes that end up being passed on in the hectic pace of our daily life, and that can ultimately become the deciding factor between war and peace. I myself have twice witnessed reporting that fatally twisted a UN investigation's scientific facts to read the opposite of what they should have been, consequently providing the warmongers – unwittingly and unintentionally – with plenty of fodder.

'Some activities may still be ongoing . . .'

The first example of this took place in Iran. On 8 November 2011, the International Atomic Energy Agency (IAEA) published a report on Iran's nuclear programme.[74] The media were gushing with superlatives, and they all agreed that Iran was on the verge of building a bomb. The German paper *Bild* went as far as asking whether the mullahs' 'nuclear missiles could even reach us'.[75] Fear was rife.

The Israeli president at the time, Shimon Peres, threatened that the prospect of his country attacking Iran's nuclear facilities was 'more and more likely'. In the US, there was open talk of a 'regime change' in Tehran. Words were followed by concrete steps; Barack Obama, as US president, imposed new sanctions on Iran. The government in Tehran responded with a large-scale manoeuvre and threatened to block the Strait of Hormuz. War was in the air.

At the time, I was on the parliamentary Foreign Affairs Committee and I needed to take a closer look at the IAEA report. I'm no nuclear expert, but at least I had written comparable reports for the UN Security Council and had a rough idea of how to read a report of that kind. In the end, I worked through it meticulously word by word several times and found ... nothing, absolutely nothing, nothing at all that would indicate an acute Iranian nuclear bomb threat. Everything in the report said unequivocally that Iran had discontinued a potential nuclear weapons programme years earlier.

How could it be that the world's press had been claiming exactly the opposite for days on end, and that there were open threats of bombing raids and a violent change of government? I was shocked, and I still am to this day: for me this story is a cautionary example of how professional distortion of facts, or 'spin doctoring', works. 'Spin' is the twist used to sell a certain story so that bad news is turned into good news, for example: have arms exports increased in the last year? Yes, but ... in comparison to the last ten years, they have fallen.

Converting a fact into its opposite, preferably without the need to lie, is the ultimate challenge in political communication. And unfortunately, it worked very well in the case of the November 2011 IAEA report. To understand exactly what happened, we need to dig a little deeper into the IAEA report. Basically, the report made three important statements.

First, it painted a clear picture of the period up to 2003. There was a military nuclear weapons programme in Iran until then. The report was very convincing on this point, even though Iran denies it to this day and dismisses it as fake news. I consider it to be verified and well documented. Iran was building a bomb – until 2003. But the programme was discontinued after that.

Second, the IAEA had precisely one indication of potential weapons-related activity in Iran in the period after 2003. It was a publication at an international conference in 2005 on what are known as 'bridge wire detonators'. They are very special high-precision detonators for explosives, which are indispensable for the construction of an atomic bomb and have very few civil applications. However, one thing immediately catches the eye here: this work was published internationally. From this, we cannot deduce that Iran has a top-secret nuclear weapons programme: on the contrary, it's obvious that nothing's secret (any more). It is very likely that in this case, results from the time before 2003, from the nuclear programme that was secret back then, were being published. This is a pattern that is familiar to us from other weapons programmes. In the mid-1990s, for example, Russian biologists published research results that clearly came from the Soviet Union's biological weapons programme, which was discontinued in 1992. In scientific circles, there is a very simple mechanism behind this: only scientists who have papers published are taken seriously, and if your work in the former weapons programme has been discontinued, you need a new job – and so you're naturally going to try to get as much published as possible. Consequently, the publication about the ominous 'bridge wire detonators' in 2005 is instead a clear indication that Iran was *not* maintaining a nuclear bomb programme at that time.

Third, the IAEA report contained two further references to potential research in Iran that could also be used for nuclear weapons. They involved neutron sources and spherical uranium components. They may or may not have been dangerous, but they were actually irrelevant, because the problem with these clues was their source: 'information from member states', or, in plain English, intelligence services. We know that information from intelligence services can be taken with a pinch of salt. The nature of information from intelligence services is that it isn't usually independently verifiable outside these services. It can be right or wrong, and sometimes it is deliberately untrue. Scepticism is therefore essential. In any case, a UN organisation like the IAEA cannot base a theory about potential nuclear weapons activities in Iran solely on sources of this kind. By being the mouthpiece of intelligence services, it's a discredit to itself.

The IAEA was aware of this, and therefore came to the very vague conclusion at the end of its report: 'some activities may still be ongoing'. Deducing from this that Iran is on the verge of building the bomb and that nuclear missiles could hit us here in Europe is absurd.

Of course, I was plagued by self-doubt. If hundreds of cars are coming towards you on the motorway, it is entirely possible that you could be on the wrong side of the road. Maybe the way the world press interpreted it was right and my way was wrong? To be absolutely certain, I went to Vienna straight away and asked the IAEA directly about it. My status as a member of parliament and, above all, my history as a UN weapons inspector helped with this; in many ways it was a conversation between former colleagues. What I learned from the IAEA staff in Vienna confirmed my suspicions, but I hadn't expected it to be so unambiguous and clear: of course Iran had stopped the weapons programme in 2003, *everyone* knew that – the German Federal Intelligence Service, the CIA, even Mossad, according to what the IAEA staff were telling me explicitly. This was also in line with a publication by the US government, which had taken exactly this stance in its public 'National Intelligence Estimate' in 2007: Iran's nuclear weapons programme was discontinued in 2003.[76]

Spin doctors at work

If all this is so clear, how could there be a complete distortion of the facts in public and, as a result, very real escalation?

To understand, we have to go back a few days. Certain media were apparently privy to the IAEA report before it was officially published. They were already releasing reports with the spin in question before 8 November 2011. This is a really simple method often used successfully by spin doctors to influence the tone of a report: a sought-after piece of information is given to individual journalists ahead of time and as exclusively as possible, sent out with their own government-official comments which dictate how it is interpreted.

For instance, on 7 November 2011, the *Los Angeles Times* came up with a long article that set the tone for the coverage that followed. Even the headline was very clear: 'Iran has technical means to make nuclear bomb, IAEA says'.[77] The newspaper doesn't refer directly to the report once in the entire article, but only to unnamed officials who would be aware of the report. In this way, the *Los Angeles Times* made sure it was unassailable, but in the process, it consciously and willingly carried out the business of the US government members who had a vested interest in the 'Iran has the bomb' story.

The newspaper also immediately launched another legend that would set the tone of the discussion for a long time: Iran could produce enough uranium to build the bomb in just six months. It didn't matter that 'six months' wasn't mentioned anywhere in the entire IAEA text: it became the key message in the following days. Iran would have the bomb in half a year.

The *Los Angeles Times* wasn't the only medium to put a spin on it in advance. This type of journalism is wrong in my view, and no amount of competitive pressure or anything else can justify it. Anyone willing to spread spin in exchange for a coveted piece of information without checking it for truthfulness is guilty of bad journalism. It's that simple. However, the question of why the incorrect interpretation prevailed, even after the report was published on 8 November, is still difficult to answer.

Once again I was too late: my analysis of the IAEA report wasn't complete until a few days later. We then discussed the report in parliament, where we were able to sow some doubts on the accepted interpretation and make sure it was on two committees' agendas – but there was no opportunity to turn the spin around. That was a very significant insight: the first headlines set the tone in the long run. That's why, when it came to my second example, a few years later, I was quick to take my place at my computer so I wouldn't be late again.

Chlorine gas over Douma?

This time it was about investigations by the Organization for the Prohibition of Chemical Weapons (OPCW) in Syria in 2018. During the Syrian civil war, there were repeated accusations from both sides that the opponents had used chemical weapons. In certain cases – such as the sarin attack on Ghouta – this was clearly confirmed by OPCW analyses.

On 7 April 2018, the Syrian regime launched heavy attacks on the rebel-held city of Douma. There was immediately an accusation that chemical weapons had been used in the air strikes. Propaganda machines started up all over the world. I myself was very sceptical at first. The reports and images were contradictory, and they were peppered with too much blatant propaganda. Over the course of the next few days, however, signs substantiating the chemical attack allegation started to emerge. Nevertheless, I wasn't entirely convinced.

The US, Great Britain and France didn't stop to ask questions; just a week later they bombed targets in Syria in response to the alleged toxic gas attack. A new escalation of the war, which was already very bloody, was on the cards. They didn't even bother to verify the alleged use of chemical weapons, but simply attacked – ironically, on the very day when the OPCW wanted to investigate the investigations on the ground. About two weeks later, however, the time had come: with the Syrian government's consent, the OPCW was able to investigate the incident in Douma. The inspectors spoke to victims and doctors, documented the situation there and took chemical samples for further analysis. Of course, the media interest worldwide was enormous, as a potential justification of the bombings by the US, Great Britain and France and the risk of further military escalation both hung on the results.

And I was right in the midst of it. At that time, as I was working freelance for the Rosa Luxemburg Foundation; I was actually involved in completely different issues, but for years I had been following anything related to biological and chemical weapons, as a little personal specialism. The OPCW had announced it would be publishing an interim report with initial findings on 6 July 2018. I'm not sure now, but I think it was due to be released at 14:00. In any case, I sat in front of my computer at the specified time to analyse the report as quickly as possible and publish the most important findings. After all, reports of this kind aren't easy to read; they are often very technical and require a certain basic knowledge. I saw my task as summarising the report as objectively as possible and giving an assessment of what the technical details meant, and as quickly as possible. I didn't want to be late again, as I had been with the Iranian nuclear programme.

Then everything turned out quite differently. As if like clockwork, at the specified time the OPCW server shut down and was no longer available. For over twenty minutes I kept trying to reach the website to no avail, only to then find out that all the major media portals had already published something about it, and all in sync, with the story being that the OPCW had detected chlorine gas in Douma. Some of these articles are still online to this day.[78]

At first, I was annoyed I was so late. But then I finally managed to download the report, and I realised that all the news stories were wrong: according to the OPCW's findings, there was no chlorine gas over Douma. In its investigation, the OPCW hadn't found any nerve gases or derivative products. 'Chlorinated substances' had been identified in environmental samples, but they could have arisen in a variety of ways. The OPCW wrote clearly and unequivocally that the significance of these findings had not yet been clarified and that the investigation was ongoing. There were no new insights: it was still unclear whether poison gas had been used or not, and both versions still seemed possible.[79]

I was shocked by it all. How could it be that all the major media around the world were carrying a false report that had nothing, absolutely nothing, to do with the OPCW's findings? The suspicion was that none of them had managed to get onto the OPCW website, and like me, had no access to the report themselves, relying instead on another source.

Later, we were able to piece things together and work out that one of the bigger international news agencies had probably sent out a report shortly after 14:00 with the key statement 'UN inspection finds chlorine gas in Douma'. Most editors had presumably simply picked up the story without even looking at the original report (or being able to do so). Some of them were corrected later, but the tone was set: toxic gas over Douma, the West's bombing raids obviously justified, and on to new offensives. The ground was prepared for further military escalation.

There's no point in speculating whether the agency simply made a mistake under time constraints, or whether someone deliberately slipped in this misinterpretation of the OPCW report. Even a simple mistake isn't that unlikely: the OPCW found 'chlorides' in the samples from Douma, which could easily be misread as 'chlorine'. But mistakes or not, we can see the very particular responsibility that news agencies have here. As journalistic service providers, they are there precisely to ensure that editorial offices around the world accept their news without a second thought. This kind of dramatic error, so relevant to war, in an agency report can have very far-reaching consequences.

Time constraints versus facts

But we'd be wrong to think of the press as liars. Even if just for a moment we accept the unlikely event that the agency deliberately lied for political reasons, no one lied in any of the editorial offices around the world that relied on the agency report; nor were they manipulated or brought into line. They weren't making propaganda; they were doing their jobs. They made a mistake, though, in an environment characterised by huge competitive pressure, driven not least by social media's lightning speeds. It's a structural problem of the modern media industry that speed takes precedence over fact-checking in acute situations.

In this day and age, scarcely any editorial offices can afford to wait for the OPCW report in a situation like that, when all the competitors around them will already be splashing the hot news on the front page. Integrity means work and costs money, as the long-time deputy editor of the *Frankfurter Rundschau*, Stephan Hebel, recently put it in an essay.[80] Money and time are both far too scarce in private sector media. They ultimately live off the number of clicks, and the ones who get there too late have lost.

I was fundamentally in the same position. Why else would I be sitting at the computer at 14:00 sharp, dying to lay my hands on the hot-off-the-press OPCW report in a matter of seconds? Of course, I'm committed to the truth, and I wanted to provide a substantiated, objective summary to take the political debate forward. If I'm honest, it was also about vanity, and about presenting myself as a sound scientist and politician providing reliable information. And about the battle for followers, for reach, for shares and likes – a pressure that also weighs heavily on many NGOs.

Whether or not the agency report was deliberately falsified on 6 July 2018 is something we're unlikely ever to get to the bottom of. It's more important to recognise that more restraint is needed in the media, especially in acute situations where it could be the difference between war or peace. And more integrity is needed too. Independent institutions could maybe also improve the situation by providing assistance, especially in complex and scientifically 'nerdy' situations such as UN inspections. But more on that later.

Ultimately, the OPCW investigation into Douma resulted in a tangible scandal. In 2019, the OPCW published a final report, concluding that chlorine gas had been used there. However, this claim was publicly contradicted by some OPCW inspectors, who couldn't find sufficient evidence of chlorine gas in Douma. The dispute has never been resolved.

True words instead of weapons

The question remains: what should be done? What should we do when words become weapons, when misinformation suddenly becomes the cause of war? We have the tool of UN inspections, which could fulfil a very significant peacekeeping function, and yet they repeatedly fail, all because of the realities of the media industry. The IAEA report could have eased the international situation in November 2011, but instead there was suddenly a very genuine threat of war with Iran.

The likelihood of being misreported stems largely from the complexity of UN inspections – the reports are often turgid and scientific. It takes a great deal of experience not to fall prey to hasty conclusions or targeted misinformation. One potential solution could be something like a disarmament observatory at the interface between science and the media: a small institution providing the scientific expertise required to analyse UN inspections and/or disarmament initiatives. The most practical approach would be for several media outlets and academic institutions to work in partnership, to ensure both independence and proximity to journalists. It wouldn't be a matter of analysing or evaluating UN reports, but simply 'translating' them for laypeople, and putting them in a political context. All UN inspections have to be written in an extremely factual way because they are commissioned by all the UN's member states and they cannot therefore take a side in any way, in terms of the language used. Often the reports don't contain any concrete conclusions because they could be too politically sensitive for certain member states. There's also, of course, pressure from the larger member states to avoid certain formulations that don't suit them politically.

As a result, inspection reports are often a presentation of the scientific facts, with no comment on them whatsoever. That's all well and good, but it naturally leaves questions unanswered. The simple knowledge that chlorine and chloride are different substances is probably not that widespread in the world's newsrooms. Or here's another example: if the UN team sent samples to two laboratories and they came to different conclusions, this is exactly how a UN report would present it. But what does that mean for us now? Yes? No? Unclear? Maybe? Or go to a third laboratory? Explaining all this and putting it in a political context could be a very helpful service for the media. Putting things into context mustn't entail drawing political conclusions from them, though – that's what the media are there for.

Maybe it's naive, but I'm convinced an observatory like this could make all the difference in acute situations, once it's earned the status of a reliable and neutral source. Liaising with a renowned scientific institute of peace research would certainly be helpful. I'd like to think that the first thing that reputable editors, at least, would do is find out what the neutral experts have to say, even in tense situations where time is key. And an observatory of this kind would also be more likely to negate any spin out there – more than a run-of-the-mill politician (especially from the left) might do, in any case.

9

Arms exports out of control

'Low cost to kill'

For many years as a member of parliament, I was on the trail of scandals involving German arms exports. Mostly from my desk, but sometimes outside in the real world too. Arms trade fairs are particularly bizarre experiences. I've twice attended IDEX, probably the world's biggest arms fair, in Abu Dhabi, where the deadliest weapons are advertised as a matter of course. At normal trade fairs, it might be tractors or sewing machines, but here it's tanks and rockets. There's a queue of boys at the Dynamit Nobel stand, waiting to have a go at shooting something on a screen with a bazooka – just like at the fair, except the boys here are all in uniform.

It's bizarre, but then again not: killing is normalised here in such a brutally sober way that you end up with a nasty taste in your mouth. You're among like-minded people here, so you can simply say it as it is: 'Low cost to kill' is the punchy slogan the German arms company Rheinmetall used to advertise a laser cannon. Kill more cheaply. Anyone who writes something like that must have lost their moral compass. At moments like these my pacifist attitude can falter and I feel like smashing something up.

A Milan, gone astray

Another trip took me, along with two colleagues, to northeast Syria in January 2014, to Rojava, predominantly inhabited by Kurds. It was a region that had driven out Assad's troops in 2012, at the beginning of the Syrian civil war, and established its own government. As a progressive, democratic project, it was a particular target for the self-proclaimed Islamic State (IS) and was constantly involved in fierce fighting. Only a few days before our arrival, the Kurdish militia YPG had been fighting over the Al Yarubiyah border crossing, where we entered the area. We wanted to find out whether the fleeing IS troops had left weapons behind – and whether the weapons might have been produced in Germany. The following day, we visited one of the YPG militia's locations and spoke directly to the commander about the weapons that had been seized. He listed an entire range of arms that they'd found in Al Yarubiyah. When he mentioned 'Milan' we all pricked up our ears: the Milan missile is a Franco-German product, and every Milan contains German technology and parts manufactured in Germany. We wanted to see them. The commander made a quick phone call, and in under an hour a YPG pickup truck arrived with a Milan missile's launch tube in the back. It had been found in an abandoned IS stronghold. It seems quite unimaginable, but the terrorist organisation IS had been using German weapons to fight in Syria. How could that have happened?

We noted down the serial number; the year of construction shown on the launch tube was 1977. Back in Berlin, we made inquiries with the government. They were able to attribute this specimen to a delivery of Milan missiles via France to Syria at the end of the 1970s. A cross-reference in the Stockholm International Peace Research Institute (SIPRI) database confirmed a delivery of 4,400 Milan missiles to Syria in 1978 and 1979. We can only speculate how the weapons from the Syrian regime's arsenals ended up in the hands of a terrorist organisation. Online we found videos and photos of an incident on 3 August 2013 when Syrian rebels stormed one of Assad's ammunition depots north of Damascus and seized Milan missiles built in 1977; it's practically impossible to know whether 'our' Milan originated there or whether it came from another source.

Bloody money

War begins here, on our doorstep. This is especially true for arms exports. The easiest way to promote peace in the world is to stop fuelling war. Nevertheless, Germany is one of the largest arms exporters in the world and supplies almost every weapon to almost every country, almost wantonly. In 2022, the British government approved arms exports to the value of £9.1 billion.

That's £9.1 billion too much. There is blood on every single one of those bank notes. Let's not kid ourselves: many of these weapons find their war, sometimes directly, sometimes in a roundabout way, sometimes only 35 years later, like the Milan missile in northern Syria. They find their war, they are used, and people die. Governments' assertions that arms will only be exported to reliable partners are in reality impossible to confirm. Scarcely anything is monitored once a weapon has been shipped.[81]

After that, it's out of sight, out of mind. There are practically no checks – or what are known as 'post-shipment controls' – to ensure that the weapons actually stay where they were originally sent. Takeaway stands are monitored better than arms exports – at least every now and then a government representative actually goes to the stand and makes sure the fryer oil isn't past it. With exported weapons, no one checks to see where they end up.

So it's not surprising that imported weapons crop up in countless wars. For many years, we've evaluated images and videos of the fighting in pretty much every armed conflict worldwide, and almost every time we could spot German weapons. 'We', in this case, was our team in parliament; I was a member of it from 2009 to 2017. I myself would be quite lost when it comes to recognising a German weapon on a shaky YouTube video, but two colleagues of mine were extremely good at it. The Milan appeared again and again, for example in 2009 with Sunni rebels in Iraq, in 2011 with rebels in Libya and in 2012 in an arms shipment for Syrian rebels.

But we also don't have to look far. Even our closest partners don't give a damn about the end-user declarations and blithely violate German export law. There's the US, for example: the company Sig Sauer, based in Schleswig-Holstein, supplied tens of thousands of pistols to the States between 2009 and 2011. From there, they were immediately sent on to Colombia, although the US submitted an end-user declaration agreeing that these weapons would remain in the US and not be sent anywhere else. So in this instance, the German licensing law was shamelessly and knowingly violated.[82]

Unfortunately, it's a fact: almost every weapon finds its war. The German government knows this too, although it has its own reasons for the many deals it approves; more on that later. For years, it's been trying to justify these shameful exports with fresh excuses. Let's take a closer look at four of these attempts to justify itself.

Excuse 1: No weapons will be supplied to war or crisis zones

Did you believe that? I did, for decades, before I took a closer look at arms exports. However, there's no regulation of this, and there never has been. Something the former Minister of Defence and CSU (Christian Social Union) hardliner Franz-Josef Strauss once said gets to the heart of the problem: 'I really don't understand why weapons are needed in areas where there isn't tension.'[83] He was clearly right. It goes without saying that weapons are supplied to places where they're urgently needed: to countries that are at war, or are preparing for it.

According to the German War Weapons Control Act, an arms export may not be approved if 'there is a risk that the weapons will be used in an act that disturbs the peace, in particular in a war of aggression'. But as long as the German government classifies even the worst wars as peacemaking measures or self-defence, they are not considered to be 'disturbing the peace', for instance the US's attack on Iraq in 2003, which violated international law but which, in the German government's view, was an act of self-defence in the fight against terror. Arms exports to the US? No problem. Nowhere is it written in any German law or in the commitments the government has agreed to that exports may not be made to war or crisis zones.

Excuse 2: If we don't supply them, others will

This is the defence I've probably heard most often. If we ban all arms exports, we might have a clean slate, but nothing would change in the world; other countries would step in immediately. At first glance, this is true, of course: as soon as one country stops selling assault rifles, buyers will turn to other countries, for example Belgium or the US. Nevertheless, this argument is wrong and, above all, immoral. Two wrongs don't make a right. I don't have to sell drugs just because my neighbours do. The consequences of our own actions can't be wiped clean by pointing at other people.

Politically, this excuse is a disgrace. Plenty would change in the world if one country were to ban all arms exports. It would be such a strong signal to the world if one of the largest arms exporters suddenly stopped. A ban in one country could be the first in a line of dominoes. Others would follow, coming under greater pressure in their own countries. They could no longer claim that everyone else was doing the same. The world is only changed by those who lead the way.

This isn't simply theory or unrealistic wishful thinking – it's already happened in real life. For years, the UN argued fruitlessly about a ban on landmines. Large countries such as China, the US and Russia didn't want them banned. Then some smaller countries broke ranks and enforced their own complete landmine ban in the Ottawa Convention. Although the major countries haven't yet ratified this treaty, weapons of this kind are now banned worldwide. Even the US largely adheres to the landmine ban due to international pressure. As soon as cluster munitions or landmines are used anywhere in the world, there's a global outcry – a tangible expression of the norm set by individual countries taking the first step. That's what it's all about, and that's why bans on arms exports are essential: so that at some point, *any* arms export from *any* country will be outlawed.

Excuse 3: So many jobs depend on it

Why do we always hear this argument from people who don't normally give two hoots about the wellbeing of the unemployed? When the UK retailer BHS went into administration in 2016, around 11,000 people lost their jobs. Was anyone in the government interested? There was no help; the story went that it was just capitalism at work.[84]

Jobs in the arms industry, on the other hand, are sacrosanct; they must be preserved come what may, even if people die as a result in other places. Yet we're talking about a negligible economic sector here. The economic value of arms exports is almost insignificant. According to CAAT, Campaign Against Arms Trade, weapons exports formed just 1.4 per cent of all British exports.[85] Even in 2022, when exports to Ukraine increased this amount significantly, spirits and liqueurs exports were of similar importance for the British export industry (9.1 billion to 7.6 billion)[86] Compared to cars, gas turbines and pharmaceuticals, arms exports are of minor importance for the British economy.[87]

ADS Group Limited, representing 1,000 companies in the aerospace, defence, security and space sectors, maintained that these three sectors provide 427,500 direct jobs;[88] the UK government claimed in 2024 that its defence spending 'supports around 434,000 jobs across the UK, with around 239,000 of those supported by industry across the UK'.[89] As we can neither trust the sector itself nor the government with their shared interest in highlighting the importance of an unpopular industry, the numbers should be viewed with caution. CAAT estimates that the real numbers are much lower: '170,000 jobs in the UK arms industry: 115,000 at the Ministry of Defence, and 55,000 in company arms exports.'[90] And how many of these jobs depend on exports is almost impossible to estimate.

However, whatever the number, if arms exports were banned, people would lose their jobs, and something would need to counter that: there's someone behind every single job with a personal story, someone who must be taken seriously. One possible solution could be *conversion*, a transition from military to civil production and, with it, the preservation of jobs. It's not my idea, nor a left-wing invention; it's actually 2,000 years old. In the Bible, it's broken down to the simple phrase 'swords into ploughshares'! Interestingly, some of today's arms producers have done the reverse: the tank manufacturer Krauss-Maffei-Wegmann, for example, started out making railway wagons and locomotives – conversion, but the wrong way round.

The concept of conversion was widespread in Western Europe in the 1970s and 1980s. In the UK, the 'Lucas Plan', a conversion paper developed by workers of the Lucas Aerospace Cooperation in 1976, is still an important reference point, even today.[91]

In any discussion of conversion in the arms industry, there's one thing that mustn't be overlooked: many other companies are also facing similar issues because their products are no longer needed. I'm thinking back to an event when, at some point in the debate about arms conversion, a man stood up in a rage and said he couldn't listen to any more of the arms industry's whingeing. He worked at Heidelberg, a major global brand making printing presses, which was facing problems as a result of digitisation. His company had been in constant conversion for years, and yet no one was talking about it. Why on earth should there be state aid for arms manufacturers?

Excuse 4: Arms exports help to stabilise countries and regions

Angela Merkel really spelled this argument out during her time as Chancellor; at times it was even known as the 'Merkel doctrine'. The theory is that exporting arms to other countries helps them protect themselves, ensuring stability in these countries and, as a result, in the world.

It's a weak argument, if only because Germany has often armed both sides of a conflict at the same time. The UK, for example, infamously armed both sides in the bloody Iraq-Iran war in the 1980s.[92] Similarly, all South American countries have bought submarines from Germany in recent decades in order to 'protect themselves from each other'. It's an absurd situation: the mutual threat among the countries would be just the same if they'd all refrained from arming their navies. And anyway, there would be much greater stability because the potential for error and destruction would be lower. There's only one winner in this game: the arms industry. The same applies to arms exports to Greece and Turkey. The two arch-enemies have been arming themselves against each other for decades. And according to SIPRI statistics, they were the first and second biggest German weapons customers in the years 2000 to 2015. Germany has armed the two countries against each other, and then claims to call this security policy?

It's absurd: one country arming itself almost always leads to that country's potential opponents feeling threatened and then going on to arm themselves too. This creates both arms races and far more complex threatening scenarios. Stability doesn't come from the barrel of a gun; it comes from democratic governance and a cooperative security policy. Arms exports have nothing to do with stability.

Arms exports as a foreign policy tool

But why do they do it? There are so many, so obviously good arguments against arms exports, and yet they're always approved. The arms industry can hardly take the blame for this. It lives off the death of other people. That's its job. And that's bad enough. But why do governments keep approving more and more new arms exports, over and over, when it scarcely has any economic relevance, but is so obviously reprehensible, both morally and politically?

The first explanation is, of course, lobbying from the arms sector. Yes, it happens, but I think its actual influence is limited. The arms industry's no longer the economic heavyweight it may have been 100 years ago, and other sectors find it easier to get governments' attention.

But we don't have to look that far up the ladder: most decisions in Germany are made much further down, by officials in the Ministry for Economic Affairs, which is responsible for controlling arms exports. 'No' is a word almost never uttered here. In fact, over ten thousand applications for arms exports are submitted every year, of which an average of around one hundred are rejected. So the system defaults to 'yes' – and that's how it's meant to be. I only really understood this after my time in parliament, during a trial in court.

In 2018, several Heckler & Koch employees stood trial for alleged violations of export regulations. One of the witnesses was a head of department in the Ministry for Economic Affairs. At the time, he was in charge of arms exports control. During the trial, he actually said that his ministry was called the 'Ministry *for* Economic Affairs' and therefore had 'an interest in ensuring this renowned manufacturer... can survive economically'.[93] That's a clear message. You don't often hear that much honesty, but that's probably exactly how it is: not controlling the economy but supporting it – that's what the ministry sees as its task. Even when it comes to arms exports.

This attitude is also widespread within ministry management. There, too, there is a vested interest in arms exports. It's never admitted publicly, but it's often put into practice: arms exports as a foreign policy tool. If good relations with country X are considered strategically important, supplying a coveted weapon can help to nurture these relationships. Or if major investment projects in the civilian sector – for instance constructing a metro system, developing electricity or phone networks – are connected by a client to the supply of armaments, that's just another way it gets done. It's no coincidence that the oil producer Saudi Arabia is one of the largest recipients of British and German weapons. You want the oil, and you want the big contracts ... and before you know it, all the moral barriers come down. This is where the 'value-driven foreign policy' quickly finds its limits.

Chemicals for the Syrian toxic gas programme

As well as armaments, there's another sector that deserves special attention: commodities known as 'dual-use' goods. These are things that can be used both in civilian and military applications. They might be, for example, electronic components that can be used in solar power systems, or in uranium production. Dual-use goods are also controlled and if there's any suspicion of military misuse, they aren't given an export licence. The EU keeps long lists of these goods. So they are subject to controls – but they still sometimes get through, even if there are suspicions of misuse.

I've already spoken of the sarin attack in Ghouta near Damascus in 2013, in the chapter on weapons inspections. The West was already aware that the Syrian regime was running a chemical weapons programme which included sarin production. When the attack in Ghouta became public knowledge, we in parliament wondered whether German industry might have been involved. It wouldn't be unheard of; we know from the UN inspections in Iraq that Saddam Hussein's chemical weapons facilities were largely built by German companies. There was the same suspicion with Libya too; the *New York Times* provocatively called it 'Auschwitz in the Sand' at the time.

The facilities were one thing; the household chemicals used to synthesise the deadly nerve gas were another. Fluorides, for example, are used in sarin production. We all know fluorides from toothpaste advertising; they are typical dual-use substances, sometimes used for peaceful purposes, at other times for lethal sarin.

So after the attack in Ghouta, we set off on a search and combed through every possible source for clues to shipments that might have been sensitive. We found what we were looking for at the UN. The UN Comtrade is a very useful database that lists all imports and exports worldwide. It is based on each country's customs data, and it's usually quite reliable. It's possible to search for specific product groups or individual items with customs codes that are standardised worldwide. We focused on the code 282611, which signifies certain fluorides. To our amazement – and horror – there were several hits. According to the UN database, Germany had repeatedly supplied fluorides to Syria, even in the 2000s. It was hard to believe: everyone knew about Syria's sarin programme. Even I knew about it, although I didn't (and still don't) have secret service clearance. Nevertheless, the German government knowingly supplied this essential precursor substance to Syria, possibly even directly to the chemical weapons programme. It couldn't be true.

To rule out any doubt, we asked the German government directly. It was forced to admit that the highly dangerous chemicals had been supplied to Syria until 2011, *with* the government's permission – since 1998, a total of 292.6 tonnes of fluorides worth €504,015.[94] And it got worse. In the course of our research, it turned out that Germany had approved these sensitive exports although other Western countries had repeatedly refused to do so, for good reason. The UK, for example, also shipped some chemicals to Syria that were used for sarin production – but this practice ended in the late 1980s.[95] Everyone involved knew that Assad was maintaining a widespread chemical weapons programme and that the fluorides could have been used for it. Other countries refused, but Germany supplied them anyway, in the process undermining an international export control agreement.

Why did the German government do this? It can scarcely have been about money; €504,015 is completely irrelevant from a macroeconomic point of view, and not even the Free Democratic Party, known for its passion for the free market, would break international agreements for that. Neither was it an oversight among less senior officials. On the contrary. We were able to prove that the decision had been made at the very top, and approved by a state secretary in the Foreign Ministry.[96]

We can only speculate about the reasons. We had an inkling that it may have had something to do with the good relationship traditionally maintained by the Federal Intelligence Service (BND) with Syria. In 2002, BND officers were allowed to be present during the interrogation of a German Syrian in Syria, and even then there were suspicions about a deal between Syria and the German government. Whether there was a deal, what exactly its content was, and exactly how the fluorides were handled is, to me, still an open question today.

How can all this be changed?

The only way to combat escalating German arms exports is by imposing clear bans, with no exceptions. If the rules aren't crystal clear, or if they allow for exceptions or a certain amount of discretion, arms exports will continue to grow. This is the sober realisation that dawned on the first coalition between the Social Democrats and the Greens in

Germany. When they came to power in 1998, both parties wanted to bring about drastic limitations on weapons exports. I'm certain they were serious about this issue; they weren't just playing to the gallery. They developed new 'political principles' for the control of arms exports, with the aim of restricting them as much as possible.

At first glance, these principles look great: human rights should play an important role, as should sustainable development; all the good intentions in the world are there. Only in exceptional cases were weapons to be delivered to 'third countries', in other words countries outside the EU or NATO, or comparable countries such as Japan. In reality, these principles didn't change a thing; arms exports even increased under that coalition government, and shipments to third countries are still not the exception but the rule. The system is still set to 'yes', the ministry in charge of the controls sees itself as an advocate for the economy and the Foreign Ministry waves through exports to keep significant partners in line.

This 'yes ... no ... maybe' approach has failed across the board. That is why *clearly defined bans* are needed, enshrined in law and enforceable. It wouldn't even be that unheard of: Japan has shown us the way. For many decades, there was an outright ban on Japanese arms exports, and not even their closest allies received a thing from them. It hasn't really harmed the country in any way.

The problem is that every government – no matter which parties are in charge – is reluctant to impose restrictions on itself, especially not now in the light of the military aid sent to Ukraine to counter the Russian invasion. In conversations with MPs from governing parties, again and again I had to listen to the argument that exemptions are absolutely essential for very particular extreme situations, because we shouldn't incapacitate ourselves by enforcing an outright export ban, and the ban would have to apply to arms for Ukraine too; more on that later. From my point of view, there would be a very simple solution for this: any exemption would have to be very strictly regulated, and safeguarded so it would only be used in extreme, exceptional situations. This could be ensured by a clause stating, for example, that any exemption must be subject to debate and passed individually by parliament. Parliamentary debate is crucial because hundreds of resolutions can be made in a few minutes, with long lists that are voted on at the drop of a hat. However, debating equals time, and that's scarce in parliament. No government would be able to simply take any old arms export to parliament: it would have to be restricted to an absolute minimum and each one would need specific justification of why it might be so particularly important.

Realistically, a universal ban won't happen overnight, but it can be done, step by step. The first, most important step would be a ban on the export of small arms and of entire arms factories. Small arms are weapons that can be transported by one person alone: assault rifles, rocket-propelled grenades, hand grenades. These, as former UN Secretary-General Kofi Annan once said, are the weapons of mass destruction of our time. In fact, up to 90 per cent of all war victims are killed not by missiles or tanks, but by small arms. Small arms are also extremely portable and can be passed from war to war. Especially from the victims' perspective, an export ban on small arms is urgently needed.

Equally important and urgent is an export ban on weapons factories sold on a turnkey basis, including machines, production documents and training. Once the factory's been built, the country in question can produce certain weapons or ammunition for years on end. If the political situation in the country changes, arms factories like these can become a real problem. This is what happened in Iran, which was given a complete G3 assault rifle factory by Germany in the 1960s. Then came the Islamic Revolution in 1979, and Iran became the West's arch enemy – and cheerfully carried on producing assault rifles with German technology. Exporting complete arms factories equates to a total loss of control over the weapons produced in them.

Legally, these bans would have to be enshrined in arms export law. The adoption of a law of this kind was written into the 2021 German coalition agreement. It sounds good, but a lot depends on exactly what it entails. If it's simply an adoption of the same old soft rules with all their exceptions, there would be little change. The first drafts aren't particularly promising.

New regulation is also essential for dual-use goods, so that a situation like the fluorides for Syria can never happen again. There is a fairly simple solution for this: countries that are not party to the Chemical Weapons Convention should no longer be allowed to receive dual-use chemicals at all. There would be no more risk of misuse. There would be no more toothpaste production either – they'd have to import their toothpaste, or else join the Chemical Weapons Convention.

10

Supplying arms or prioritising a civil approach?

As well as the routine commercial arms exports all over the world, there are always special situations where governments supply weapons directly to support one side in a war, for example to Ukraine since 2022, or to Kurdistan in 2014. These two different circumstances sometimes get mixed up in political discussions, and it's also difficult to distinguish between them linguistically. From my point of view, it's useful to make a distinction between *exporting* arms and *supplying* arms. We discussed exporting arms in detail in the previous chapter: other countries order weapons from a German arms company, the German government approves the shipment and then the weapons are sold. Supplying arms means direct war support with weapons, supplied by the government, often by the armed forces and usually with no payment involved. This is a useful distinction because arms are supplied directly for a war in which a country wants to intervene. It's a complex situation, with many good arguments for and against it – and it needs to be assessed quite differently from commercial arms exports.

Many countries have been very divided over the pros and cons of supplying arms to Ukraine over the past two years, and many people are still uncertain about it now. It's not helped by the fact that there are no easy answers; we have to choose between a rock and a hard place. Personally, I'm against supplying arms. I'm not a radical pacifist who would never, ever take up arms. The atrocities of Nazi Germany and the liberation by the Allies are still far too fresh in my mind. My pacifism can be defined by the principle of prioritising a civil approach: always starting by looking for non-military solutions, which must take precedence over everything else. And I'm quite sure that there can almost always be nonviolent paths to peace, paths that can often be even faster and more effective than weapons.

My philosophy – prioritising a civil approach and looking for peaceful alternatives – can best be illustrated with the example of the arms supplied to Kurdistan in 2014.

Weapons for Kurdistan

Late at night on 25 September 2014, I was standing in Erbil airport in northern Iraq. Away from the airfield, next to an old cargo terminal, there were several television crews and a dozen or so German journalists. Next to us, British and American forces were busy, despite it being so late. At precisely 23:12, an old C130 Hercules transport plane touched down and taxied towards us, its massive propellers gradually slowing. On board were three pallets of G3 assault rifles and bazookas. They were for the Kurdish autonomous region's battle against the terrorist militia Islamic State (IS) and had been donated by the armed forces. To me it was wrong – a conviction that troubled me to my core.

At the beginning of the year, I'd visited Rojava, the Kurdish self-governed area in northern Syria – genuinely a model project for leftists, a kind of socialist council-based republic in the midst of the Syrian civil war. It was under attack from Turkey and its allied jihadist militias, and it was isolated worldwide because it didn't fit into any of the classic East–West pigeonholes. In the fight against IS, there was something the Kurdish militias asked for more than anything else: weapons. Solidarity with Rojava was great, not only from the German government, but also and especially from many leftists in Germany who were wholeheartedly in favour of supplying arms to Kurdistan.

My question wasn't whether supplying arms is right or wrong in principle. I was concerned with this individual case: what kind of help from the German government would be most effective in supporting the Kurdish militias in the fight against IS? What non-military solutions could there be? To me, it was all about prioritising a civil approach.

When it came to weapons for Kurdistan, the question was easy to answer. In essence, you could say that weapons were a cheap substitute for genuine politics, so that German financial interests in the Gulf and the close friendship with Turkish President Erdoğan weren't jeopardised. There would have been alternatives, and not just in hindsight but precisely at the time the German government was deciding to supply weapons. But first things first . . .

At that time, in 2014, monetary donations were one of the biggest sources of funding for IS – donations that came mainly from the Gulf states, from rich Islamist private individuals and handled by religious foundations. There had already been UN resolutions to block these financial channels, decisively weakening IS. Without money, there are no weapons, no fighters and no victories. All the world's countries were called upon to starve this organisation of donations.

Almost by chance, I was in Qatar in February 2015, on the trail of the worst working conditions in stadium construction sites for the 2022 men's World Cup. In the course of my research, I met the Qatari Minister of Labour, accompanied by the German ambassador. There was a memorable moment: three times, the minister mentioned almost in passing that he was also responsible for religious donations. When he first mentioned it, the ambassador ignored him; the second time she was irritated, and when it happened a third time she exclaimed in surprise: 'Oh goodness, I didn't know that.' The

Qatari minister replied dryly that he'd noticed that unlike her, her US counterpart visited him every week, because religious donations were a particular focus of world attention. Despite the UN resolution, and despite daily assurances from the German government that it really was doing everything humanly possible to bring down IS, the German ambassador wasn't even aware who in Qatar was responsible for the money-laundering trusts supporting IS. Or did she not want to know?

Prioritising the economy

When I told this story in a TV discussion a few weeks later, another guest, a member of parliament from the Christian Democratic Union, promptly said that we had to be careful with Qatar – after all, they owned 17 per cent of VW's shares.

It was clear that the priority lay in a number: 17 per cent of VW's shares. That was more important than the fight against the mob of IS murderers, more important than the lives of the Kurds in northern Syria. Apparently, this wasn't just an individual member of parliament's opinion. Ultimately the government took exactly the same line: not putting pressure on as important an economic partner as Qatar, but instead supplying arms to the people who were being attacked with Qatar's support. It was a hopeless undertaking, because compared to the arms IS was able to purchase with the help of the millions it was constantly receiving from the Gulf states, the arms supplied to the Kurds were no more than a drop in the ocean. For Germany, however, it was cheaper than endangering economic relations with Qatar. And more effective in the public eye.

Back then, in 2014, there would have been another possibility to severely disrupt IS's advance by non-military means. At the time, there was fairly candid support for IS from the Turkish government in Ankara. The IS area in northern Syria bordered Turkey for hundreds of kilometres, and every night, international IS terrorist fighters were able to travel from Turkey to the combat zone with their weapons. Thousands and thousands of Islamists from all over the world took the route through Turkey, as was later proved by the entry stamps in their passports. Behind this was Turkey's interest in preventing an unwelcome Kurdish self-governed area in northern Syria, which still stands to this day. Some companies in Turkey were also making good money by trading Syrian oil, which IS was illegally smuggling into Turkey.

And again in this instance, the armed forces wouldn't have been able to supply the Kurds with as many weapons as the opposing terrorist organisation were amassing via Turkey every night. Once again, the political costs were spared. Pressure on the Turkish president would have been necessary, and it might have risked the traditionally very good relationship between Germany and Turkey. So it's preferable to supply weapons; it doesn't cost a thing, politically at least.

This experience from 2014 deeply influenced my thinking about supplying arms to Ukraine. Always look at what is civilly possible first, without resorting to the military.

The man with the hammer

There are so many strong arguments against supplying arms. One of the most important is that weapons almost always fall into the wrong hands at some point. Once weapons have crossed national borders, there's no effective control over where they end up. We know from small arms, assault rifles and anti-tank missiles in particular that they're sometimes passed on from war to war for decades, like the Milan missiles we had found in the region only a few months earlier. And, of course, that's exactly what happened in autumn 2014: as soon as the weapons arrived with the Kurdish militias, they appeared on the local black market, freely available for anyone involved in the war. Anyone who supplies weapons to a war can never take it as read that those arms will only go to one side; the situations on the ground are far too complex for that.

The example of supplying arms to the Kurdish militias illustrates how much German foreign policy is shaped by military thinking. When it comes to foreign policy problems, it's often only military solutions that are sought. It reminds me of the well-known saying: to a man with a hammer, every problem looks like a nail. If you only have tanks up your sleeve, tanks are all you can think of.

To a man, or woman, with a tank, there's the military option – or the option of doing nothing. It's a completely bogus set of opposites, often used as a sledgehammer to beat down any pacifist position. For eight years, I had to sit and listen to more and more insults in parliament. Among other things, I was accused of abandoning the oppressed girls in Afghanistan if I voted against the armed forces' mission: propaganda that's as nasty as it is cunning, as it puts you on the defensive. It's *you* who then has to show what the alternatives might be. It's *you* who has to prove that they can work – whereas no one expects proof of genuine military effectiveness from the men and women with the tanks. A tank can get stuff done, everyone assumes. Peaceful paths are often more complex and much more difficult to imagine.

Pacifism: for peace, but not helpless

Even in the middle of the fierce war in Afghanistan, there were wonderful examples of how construction can work – even to the extent of a girls' school being built in the middle of Taliban territory – if you're not looking at it through military eyes. My first trip as a member of parliament took me to Afghanistan. Among other things, we were in Kabul for political talks. There, a German development worker told me this story. A few years earlier, they had been asked to work in a heavily fought-over province in southern Afghanistan. They'd been warned by all sides that the region was far too dangerous, literally: 'You'll be shot down on the spot.' But the development workers didn't let that stop them. They chose the arduous path of detailed research, had countless conversations and got to know the facts, with the help of Afghan experts: who's actually shooting whom, and why? Who's in charge in the provinces, in each district and in the villages? On the basis of this analysis and armed with this knowledge, they were then able to talk to the right people in the villages and plan a long-term development project together with them. As all sides were on board and as they were able to respond to every side's needs, ultimately no one was shot down on the spot. One condition for it to happen, according to the development worker, was that there wasn't a single military officer present.

There are many stories like this, and not only from Afghanistan, that prove that there are so many options in between military action and inaction. We must never let ourselves fall into the trap of having to face the bogus choice between intervening militarily and doing nothing at all. It is always crucial to examine civil options as well – and in most cases we'll find that they do exist, or at least could exist – even in Ukraine. But there'll be more on that at the end of this book.

11

SANCTIONS AND THEIR SIDE EFFECTS

Some people celebrate them as the continuation of politics by peaceful means; others reject them as an economic war. Opinions differ on the issue of sanctions. This is partly because the effects and side effects of sanctions are closely linked. In the past, they've often been used with great success, but they have also been the cause of horrific disasters. The terrible sanctions on Iraq in the early 1990s, which resulted in countless deaths, are still a bad memory for many. At the other end of the scale there's the successful example in South Africa, where the global economic embargo certainly contributed to the overthrow of the apartheid regime.

Since then, there have been some fascinating findings from research into sanctions that provide clues as to what might help in which situations and what tends to backfire.[97] To get straight to the point, I think prudently used sanctions can definitely be an important factor as a means of exerting pressure to avoid or end a war. However, since they can also cause plenty of damage, prudence and foresight are immensely important in the decision for or against sanctions.

First of all, we need a brief explanation of the terms: sanctions, embargo and boycott. What are the differences? There are no clearly delineated definitions, but sanctions are commonly measures taken by nations, in contrast to boycotts, which are individual purchasing decisions. So if someone decides on a personal level not to buy fruit from South Africa, this is usually called a boycott. If a government issues an import ban on that fruit, we call it sanctions. The term 'embargo' is a special type of sanction and means comprehensive nationally imposed isolation measures against a country. If nothing enters or leaves a country, these all-encompassing sanctions can be called an embargo. There is also a whole range of sanctions with varying degrees of targeting; they might only be imposed on individual companies, sectors of the economy or individuals. Travel bans are also included in this.

An important basis for sanctions is the UN Charter. Chapters VI and VII of the Charter deal with potential measures to maintain peace (see also Chapter 5). In essence, the UN recommends a three-step process: diplomacy, sanctions, war. Sanctions fall under Article 41 of the UN Charter. It mentions the 'complete or partial interruption of economic relations' as another potential coercive measure. If we didn't have sanctions, the trio of measures would merely become two-pronged, and the pressure to move towards military action, supplying arms and foreign operations would increase.

However, it is also important to remember that sanctions are coercive measures; they can easily be abused and have fatal consequences. This makes it all the more important to debate how and under what conditions sanctions can be used in the most targeted way possible, to avoid unwanted side effects.

The Iraqi catastrophe

The fatal effects of this kind of coercive measure were particularly evident in Iraq. On 2 August 1990, the Iraqi dictator Saddam Hussein invaded the small neighbouring country of Kuwait, and only four days later the UN Security Council adopted what was probably the most comprehensive package of sanctions in its history. With Resolution 661 of 6 August, one of the darkest chapters in the United Nations' existence was set in motion. It stipulated an almost complete trade embargo, and all Iraqi imports and exports were banned. The only exceptions were 'in humanitarian circumstances, foodstuffs' and 'supplies intended strictly for medical purposes'.[98] Even food and medicines were only allowed to a limited extent – with catastrophic consequences.

UNICEF later calculated that child mortality in Iraq subsequently exploded, and up to 500,000 children died as a result of the sanctions.[99] These figures have since been put into perspective to a certain extent, as the Iraqi regime apparently exaggerated the infant mortality rate at the time. But it's ultimately irrelevant whether it was 100,000 or 500,000 children who died when we're evaluating these sanctions. The fact remains that they caused immeasurable suffering for the people of Iraq.

The Iraqi experience has created an image of sanctions that persists in the public's eyes: sanctions are intended to deliberately cause severe economic hardship so that the population rebels against the regime. This isn't the point, though: that would be a crime against humanity. It wouldn't work at all, because most of the time the opposite effect occurs: people get the feeling that now they need to stick together against the rest of the world and unite behind the regime in question. From that moment on, the regime can blame everything that goes wrong in the country on sanctions and avoid taking responsibility.

This is what happened in Iraq at that point. Saddam Hussein's regime wasn't weakened – on the contrary. Especially when sanctions are prolonged, they can lead to the regime adapting and setting up circumvention projects to procure all the goods their population needs. The regime and companies close to it benefit from this and rack up enormous amounts of influence, power and money. Saddam Hussein understood precisely how to exploit the greatest shortages for his own purposes. Loyal groups of the population received rations, even of the scarcest goods, while the hated Kurdish population in the north, for example, went empty-handed.

We're still feeling some of the effects of the misguided Iraq sanctions to this day. Dastan Jasim, an Iraqi Kurdish woman who's currently doing her doctorate on the subject at the German Institute for Global and Area Studies (GIGA) in Hamburg, has pointed out a fatal long-term effect: due to the embargo, the regime became dependent on smuggling, and particularly on some adept groups of smugglers in the border area between Iraq and Syria. As a result, they grew rich and powerful – and later became a big problem, for Iraq as well as for the entire world, when they joined the group known as Islamic State (IS), which continues to terrorise the region to this day.[100]

Although the world protested and drew attention to the country's humanitarian catastrophe, the strict sanctions were maintained for 13 long years. The US, in particular, blocked any attempt to lift sanctions in the UN Security Council.

The Iraq sanctions were certainly extreme. However, one thing is always true with sanctions: if they work, they also have side effects. There are no surgically precise sanctions that truly manage not to hurt any innocent civilians at all. Even if we're only talking about a travel ban for members of the government, other people are always affected, even if it's only the taxi driver who would have driven them to the airport.

Unwanted side effects don't just hit the country targeted by the sanctions. Neighbouring countries are soon affected economically if they lose their most significant trading partner. Sanctions could also have a severe impact on other countries on a global scale, for example if gas and oil prices go through the roof worldwide due to an import ban on fossil fuels.

So side effects are unavoidable. The goal must be to keep them to a minimum. What exactly this means is looking in detail at each individual case – and it isn't just a moral or political issue; it's a legal one too, but there'll be more on that later.

Targeted sanctions

Policy on sanctions has been subject to a rethink in view of the devastating Iraq experience, and concepts for more targeted sanctions have evolved. 'Targeted' can mean either certain economic sectors, certain people or even certain companies. A classic form of targeted sanction is the arms embargo. In an ideal world, this wouldn't be necessary at all, because there would no longer be any weapons being exported from any country anyway (see Chapter 9), but unfortunately, we're not there yet.

In a slightly extended form, targeted sanctions can affect a country's entire war capability by no longer supplying anything that could be used militarily. This also includes dual-use goods, which we've already touched on in the chapter on arms exports, for example, or engines that could be fitted into tanks, electronic control devices, chips or certain metals – there are plenty of dual-use goods, so this form of sanctions would only be targeted to a limited extent, as so many other civilian production chains would also be affected.

Targeted sanctions aimed at the regime's political and/or economic power base – at the heart of the beast – have particular potential. A really interesting example of this is Russia's sanctions against Turkey in 2015. Turkey had shot down a Russian fighter jet on the Turkish–Syrian border. Putin demanded an apology, and Erdoğan refused, so Putin imposed sanctions.

One of the sanctions affected the tourism sector. Russian tour operators were no longer allowed to offer trips to Turkey, and all charter flights to Turkey were suspended. This had a massive impact, as Turkey had been one of the most popular travel destinations for Russians. The dearth of Russian tourists resulting from the sanctions hit the Turkish tourism sector hard, and with it, apparently, some leading members of Erdoğan's AKP party too, whose wealth came from this industry. In this respect, the Russian tourism sanctions were targeted both in the sense that a certain industry was attacked and because at the same time they were aimed at the decision-makers in Ankara and their personal wealth. Clearly it was a very clever strategy, because only a few months later Turkey caved in, apologised profusely, and the two countries once again had their place in the sun, especially by the pool in Antalya.

Hitting the political leaders' power base is the supreme discipline when it comes to targeted sanctions. Based on this logic, the French economist Thomas Piketty presented a rather elegant idea for sanctions against Russia, as early as March 2022.[101] According to him, at the time there were around 20,000 people in Russia who were worth over ten million dollars. These multimillionaires are at the heart of the Russian business elite and a key mainstay of the Putin government. If all of them – and not just the very richest oligarchs – were put on a sanctions list, Piketty argued, then pressure could be exerted on the Kremlin, as these multimillionaires would be severely affected by their foreign assets being frozen. If an entrepreneur with a medium-sized business is deprived of his villa on a beautiful Bavarian lake, he, unlike the prominent oligarchs, won't necessarily have a second one. He's then faced with the choice of safeguarding his personal assets *or* continuing to support the Kremlin. It's not an easy choice in today's Russia, and very few would publicly revolt – but they might leave Russia, weakening the Russian economy further. At least there would be a chance of things being shaken up.

It sounds simpler than it would be in practice. For one thing, foreign authorities cannot simply freeze or confiscate goods at will, even in war; sanctions lists of this kind would have to be legally substantiated. With 20,000 individual people, it wouldn't be easy. More than anything, though, as it stands German authorities cannot confiscate villas on Bavarian lakes: they don't know who their owners ultimately are if nested shell companies are involved. A lack of transparency in the property market, and in the economic sector in general, makes it very difficult to implement targeted sanctions. One possibility could have been travel bans: then at least the villa on the lake would be out of action.

The effectiveness – or failure – of sanctions

Sanctions are useless anyway: this is a widespread view, and it's definitely related to the fact that it's not that easy to measure sanctions' success. For one thing, this is because sanctions always have an indirect effect and there's usually some kind of lateral thinking behind them. The intention is to achieve a certain economic effect in order to ultimately achieve a political goal. There are examples of sanctions where an economic effect has been felt but the desired political goal hasn't materialised. In my view, that would make it an unsuccessful sanction: the yardstick has to be an effective political change and not just some economic indicators going up or down. They are only a means to an end.

The other difficulty in evaluating sanctions is that they rarely work on their own. We're usually dealing with very complex international relations. If something changes for the better politically, it's difficult to say exactly what part the sanctions have played in this. Maybe a significant ally exerted some pressure at the same time? Maybe the target country's leadership is under pressure to change for other reasons? It's practically impossible to separate the various influences on certain economic data or political changes analytically.

It's therefore not surprising that there are often quite different assessments of the effectiveness of individual sanctions regimes in sanctions research. On one particular point, though, there is a consensus among researchers: in principle, sanctions can be effective and have achieved political results in the past. One of the standard academic works on the subject is the book *Economic Sanctions Reconsidered* by Gary Hufbauer et al., last revised in 2009.[102] After evaluating

174 sanctions regimes between 1919 and 2000, they reach the conclusion that sanctions were effective in about a third of the cases – effective in the sense that, for one thing, the political goals were achieved and, for another, the sanctions demonstrably played a part in this.

A third doesn't sound like much, but every single case is a resounding success if it means a military escalation is avoided. There's one more element that must be considered, though: as a rule, sanctions are threatened first – and it's only if the country in question fails to respond to the threat that sanctions are imposed. This means that the 'simple' cases where a country has responded to a threat and the political goal has been achieved without sanctions actually happening are often not included in these statistics.

In my view, however, the decisive issue isn't so much the precise success rate as the question of why some sanctions work and others fail. What factors determine success and failure? We can learn for the future from the answers to these questions. And with this in mind, the research provides some really interesting insights.[103]

Some results from the research are obvious: for example, sanctions are a tool used by the strong against the weak. Liechtenstein would find it hard to put Germany under economic pressure, but it would be a different story if the roles were reversed. And the closer the economic ties with the target country, the more effective the sanctions can be.

It's a very revealing insight – especially looking at the debate on Russia sanctions – that a slow, gradual tightening of sanctions isn't very likely to be effective, because the target country can adapt more easily to it. This is a contradiction to diplomatic thinking, which tends to proceed cautiously, gradually increasing gentle pressure rather than throwing everything at the problem immediately. The essence of diplomacy is always keeping communication lines open. Unfortunately, this doesn't work with sanctions; they can't be classed as diplomacy but instead as a coercive measure, and one important rule applies: either all, and fast, or nothing at all.

This can be seen with the Russia sanctions. The EU discussed a potential oil embargo for months on end, and even when it was introduced, there was a long transition period. It actually only became effective about a year after the invasion of Ukraine. In that year, Russia both earned an enormous amount of money by selling oil to the EU, financing the war in the process, and also built up a fleet of tankers for transporting Russian oil and selling it all over the world. This isn't how effective sanctions work.

Now is the time to look back and see what we could have done better. Oil sanctions should have been on the agenda in 2014, after the Russian annexation of Crimea. At the time, I was wrong about the Russian government's character, and I was still advocating an end to the Russia sanctions in 2017[104] – a big mistake, I have to admit in hindsight. The Kremlin has always taken the West's economic interests into account and relied on the fact that cheap oil and gas are more important to us than any international law. Only a quick, all-encompassing halt to all oil imports could have really surprised the Kremlin and put it under pressure.

Some sanctions researchers even go as far as saying that sanctions over long periods of time make no sense anyway. The longer they run, the more likely it is that ways will be found to circumvent them, and the more they affect civil society. If it hasn't had an effect after a year, it won't work in the long run. This contradicts the widespread myth that sanctions always take far too long to take effect. It isn't merely a theory: just look at the example of the Russia–Turkey crisis above. If we bear in mind that handling conflicts in a purely military way usually takes many bloody years before a peace solution is reached, severe economic cuts could have a much faster effect – if they're done well and offer the targeted country a clear-cut prospect of recovery.

This brings us closer to the crucial factor for a sanction's success: an end must be in sight. It's essential from the outset that the country concerned knows the precise goal that the sanctions are intended to achieve, and under what specific conditions they will be lifted. If this is formulated in detail when the sanctions are decided upon, it becomes more probable that sanctions will achieve their political goal. Only if there is a clearly defined policy for lifting the sanctions can the targeted country's government make an ongoing cost-benefit calculation: if we take step x, it's guaranteed that sanction y will be lifted. It's impossible to make a clear-cut calculation along these lines if a sanctions ruling doesn't spell out clearly when (or at what 'cost') the sanctions will be withdrawn.

It sounds so logical, but it's rarely the case in reality. The European Union's resolutions on the Russia sanctions don't even formulate clear goals; there are only vague references to earlier EU resolutions on the annexation of Crimea.

Sanctions against apartheid

The question of whether sanctions were effective or not can be answered unequivocally in the case of South Africa. Sanctions played a significant role in the downfall of the old apartheid regime in 1994 and in Nelson Mandela being elected president in the first truly free elections. There had already been a worldwide campaign against white supremacy. In some countries, activists marched into supermarkets and poured blood over fruit from South Africa. A global boycott movement was supported by civil society, and it was accompanied by state sanctions against South Africa from the mid-1980s. By the end of the 1980s, the South African economy was in crisis. When international investors withdrew, it was the last straw. There is a general consensus that the sanctions helped bring about the end of apartheid. Of course, it's hard to quantify exactly how large or small their part in it was. In South Africa, there's still a debate going on now about how much the civilian boycott movement, state sanctions and/or individual companies' withdrawals each contributed to the South African economy's collapse.

One thing in particular is certain, and it's something very distinctive: the sanctions against South Africa were supported in the country itself, mainly by those who were most affected by them. The black communities were the first to lose their jobs in the economic crisis, and yet they campaigned worldwide for the sanctions to bring the hated apartheid regime to its knees. The sanctions initially hit the wrong people, who nevertheless agreed with them; and the sanctions ultimately worked because they hit the right people.

In hindsight, the cultural and sporting sanctions against South Africa are also seen as positive – which is surprising at first glance, as cultural or academic sanctions are intrinsically counterproductive. It's often precisely the artists and academics who retain intellectual freedom even in the darkest of times, and who might still be available to the world beyond their borders. They can often be the last delicate point of contact with the outside from within a country. This is why I would oppose any cultural or scientific sanctions against Russia in the current situation. In hindsight, though, this is seen differently in relation to South Africa. A significant cornerstone of the entire apartheid ideology was the myth that the white elite was closely linked to Europe. This myth was shaken up by the cultural sanctions, and the regime began to develop bigger and bigger cracks.

Sanctions as a means of power

Unfortunately, it's more often the case that rather than using sanctions for noble causes, peace or conflict resolution, they are taken up as a hard-hitting means of power to assert vested interests with economic force. We've already seen that by their nature, sanctions can actually only be effective as a tool of the strong against the weak. And often enough, the strong act not in the interests of world peace in this context, but in their own. While the US has been imposing a total embargo on little Cuba for decades, it's had nothing to do with peace, but with destroying another economic and social model.

A look at the figures substantiates this. Of the 174 sanctions regimes investigated by Hufbauer et al., 81 were imposed by the US alone, and there were another 27 where the States joined other countries in imposing them. The Soviet Union and Russia have also been involved in 13 sanctions regimes. In this respect, it's clear that sanctions are a means of force primarily used by world powers.

In my view, though, it would be disastrous to condemn all sanctions as imperialist scheming. Exploitation and abuse exist but that doesn't mean that all sanctions are bad. It depends on the aims. Sanctions can only be the right tool when the goal is helping threatened or oppressed people – when they're under attack by another country, or when they're being exploited, oppressed or threatened in their own country, as was happening in South Africa.

However, power also works the other way around, and can evade sanctions. Even in the Russia–Ukraine war, individuals or business sectors repeatedly manage to be exempt from the sanctions because they apparently hold too much power. Here are just two concrete examples:

As of December 2022, 1,241 Russian individuals were on the EU sanctions list. Vladimir Potanin, one of the richest men in Russia and for 20 years a loyal supporter of Putin, with whom he played ice hockey, wasn't on it. I would have expected Potanin to be on the list for the very first round of sanctions. His power comes from the fact that he controls Russian nickel production and other important metals, and he's built a large battery factory in Finland in partnership with Germany's BASF. The fact that he was exempt from the sanctions is probably related to the fear of some EU car manufacturers that Potanin could cut off their supply of important metals.[105] The US put Potanin on their sanctions list at some point in December 2022, whereas the EU didn't. This is what happens if your car is more important to you than your neighbour's life.

The second is a glittering example: Antwerp is the diamond capital of the world, with an annual turnover of $36 billion from these precious stones. It's an important economic sector for the small country of Belgium, which is why the government there prevented Russian diamonds being added to the sanctions list. Diamond mining in Russia is partly in state hands, so the income from them flows directly into the Kremlin's war chest. Whoever has money has power.

What does international law say?

A common argument against sanctions is the claim that they are contrary to international law if they aren't approved by the UN Security Council. To get to the bottom of this question, in 2023 the Rosa Luxemburg Foundation commissioned a report from an expert in international law, with some interesting results.[106] The author, Hannah Kiel, concluded that the legal situation is only clear in the issue's peripheries; there is a fairly large grey area where legal interpretations diverge, partly because the geopolitical perspective in question has a certain amount of influence on how sanctions are viewed.

It's generally agreed that *arms embargoes* are legal. At the other end of the spectrum, there's a broad consensus that the extreme US sanctions regime against Cuba is contrary to international law.

It's also quite clear-cut that the UN Security Council is entitled to adopt sanctions in the event of 'threats or breaches of the peace and acts of aggression', and it has done so about thirty times in the past. It's important to note though that this only applies to the UN Security Council and not to the UN General Assembly, whose resolutions are not legally binding – although they do, of course, have significant political influence.

At this point, we also need to clarify some terminology. A distinction is often made between unilateral and multilateral sanctions. The only criterion here is a Security Council resolution: without it, sanctions are unilateral, whereas they become multilateral if a resolution is passed. Even if the entire EU and a dozen other countries impose sanctions, they are classed as unilateral if they don't come from the UN Security Council.

There is no rule in international law to prohibit unilateral sanctions in general. However, some legal regulations set clear limits on sanctions – above all when it comes to the prohibition of intervention and the observance of human rights. The prohibition of intervention means one nation may not interfere in another nation's internal affairs. Where exactly the boundary between permissible economic sanctions and the prohibition of intervention lies is highly controversial in academic debate, because sanctions by their very nature always intervene in a nation's internal affairs. What is clearer, though, is that most sanctions can have an impact on human rights, above all on the right to life, health and freedom from hunger. According to the report, it follows from this that any sanctions that lead to hunger are contrary to international law – which is why almost every current sanctions regime makes an exception for humanitarian aid.

Even if the prohibition of intervention and human rights standards are potentially being violated, sanctions can be lawful if there is appropriate justification. What is certain is that sanctions can be imposed instead of military measures, provided the conditions of the right of self-defence (Article 51 of the UN Charter) are met.

Keeping an eye on the goal

All in all, it turns out that many of the concerns over sanctions have a kernel of truth. Yes, there can be abuse of power; yes, many innocent people can be affected; and they can even be contrary to international law. Poorly devised sanctions do not work, and very badly devised sanctions can even cause serious damage – but well thought-out sanctions can be a genuine alternative to war and violence. Our starting point is the UN Charter, and the three-pronged approach of diplomacy, sanctions and war, where sanctions are a possible means of exerting pressure on the one hand without using military force on the other. Well-thought-out sanctions define clear goals together with a clear vision for their lifting, are as short and snappy as possible, are specifically directed against those responsible and their power base, and also keep unforeseen consequences to a minimum. Above all, though, good sanctions don't pursue selfish interests, but are an expression of international solidarity with the attacked, persecuted and oppressed people of this world.

12

WAR STARTS HERE. PEACE TOO

At this point, we have to talk about our own situation in Europe, and about our contribution to unrest and war worldwide. I'm not just talking about participation in war, in Afghanistan, Mali or anywhere else. We learned from Lian Gogali's example in Indonesia how closely local conflicts on the other side of the world are sometimes linked to our way of life. In her case, it was nickel for the Western car industry that fuelled the local conflicts again. For us, this means one thing above all, more than anything else: if we want to maintain peace, we have to uphold justice, and we have to work towards changing things here in our country as well. If this doesn't happen, any attempts to make peace or resolve conflicts will merely paper over the cracks and are bound to fail from the outset.

'War starts here' was the slogan used by a campaign against German arms exports. Arms exports are only the tip of the iceberg: their link to violence, war and death goes without saying. But it's not only assault rifles and hand grenades that escalate wars. Chocolate can be lethal, too.

Bitter chocolate

Maybe it's because I'm an absolute chocoholic, but for many years cocoa cultivation with all its injustices hasn't been sitting well in my stomach. The idea that my favourite chocolate is produced by exploiting child slaves enrages me, as does the fact that unfair trade in cocoa has even led directly to wars. When the civil war began in Côte d'Ivoire in 2002, it was closely linked to the fact that the plummeting global market prices for cocoa had a direct impact on the poorest rural population, resulting in violent conflicts that had been smouldering for a long time. The civil war lasted for years, with many fatalities.

But let's start at the beginning. If we buy a cheap bar of chocolate for a pound in our trusted supermarket, only seven to ten pence reaches the family in Côte d'Ivoire who grew the cocoa under the toughest conditions. Only seven to ten per cent of the retail price ends up with the farmers. They can't live on that. Their share of the profits is non-existent.[107]

To be able to live, you need to have at least what's known as a 'living income'. This should actually be quite self-evident for every job: enough to be able to purely survive, to be able to adequately feed yourself and your family. However, cocoa cultivation in Côte d'Ivoire is very far from that, with smallholder families there earning just US$196 a month, while a living income in Côte d'Ivoire is US$543 a month for an average-sized family. These figures come from INKOTA, a dynamic organisation in Berlin that's been working on global injustices for over fifty years, and paying particular attention to the injustices behind chocolate ('Make Chocolate Fair!').

It's possible to calculate very precisely how expensive cocoa would have to be on the world market to ensure families can live at least at subsistence level. INKOTA is part of an international alliance that regularly publishes the 'Cocoa Barometer', with fascinating and shocking figures about cocoa. In October 2022, a kilo of cocoa cost just US$1.30 from the farmer: no family can live on that. According to INKOTA, that price should be at least $3, in other words more than double. If we translate that to our favourite bar of chocolate, it would mean we'd have to pay just nine pence more.

The journey from a small farm in Côte d'Ivoire to our supermarket is a very long one. The middlemen, transport companies, international agricultural corporations, big players in the chocolate industry such as Nestlé and Ferrero – they all make money from the cocoa. And then there are the people who have nothing to do with the actual cocoa, who neither grow nor transport nor process it, but who simply make money from it: the speculators. Every day, there's a lot of speculation on the London Stock Exchange over food, including cocoa.

In actual fact, a stock exchange's purpose is to bring sellers and buyers together. When this happens – or so I learned at school – supply and demand determine the price. In practice, though, there are still people who speculate on falling or rising cocoa prices and regularly buy and sell large quantities of cocoa just to make huge profits from the price differences. What this looks like in real life was described very plainly by the venerable German Cocoa Trade Association in its 2020 annual report.[108] In fact, according to the association, the prices for cocoa should have been very stable that year as the harvest forecasts were good and demand was stable, so there was no reason for large price fluctuations.

However, fluctuations did occur: speculators on the stock exchange had entered certain lower and upper limits for cocoa prices in their automated systems, and the price fluctuated between them. If it fell to £1,570 per tonne, they bought. If it rose to £1,800, they sold. And they made hefty profits every time without even having seen a single cacao bean in their lives. Money that the farming families in Côte d'Ivoire are desperate for, for their livelihoods, ends up in the hands of some bankers in the City of London. From this we can only conclude that any kind of speculation with food should be banned: it costs lives.

Which brings us back to war. For many decades, cocoa was Côte d'Ivoire's most important export commodity, and more and more land was earmarked for cocoa cultivation. The boom attracted many migrant workers from neighbouring Burkina Faso. Some of them bought land and grew cocoa themselves. For a long time, smallholder family farms were protected from the hardships of the world market by government regulation and guaranteed prices, until the World Bank and the International Monetary Fund (IMF) exerted pressure in the 1990s and enforced a 'liberalisation' of the cocoa market. 'Liberal' makes it sound far too positive: it was all about dismantling the protective mechanisms for farmers, who were then defenceless against the global corporations' and speculators' shenanigans. When world market prices for cocoa plummeted in 1999, millions of farming families were dragged into the abyss and the entire country fell into a deep economic crisis.

At that point, long-standing conflicts broke out into violence – conflicts that had racism at their core, with 'real' Ivorians rejecting the migrant workers from the north. With the economic crisis, there was added competition for land and income. As a result of an attempted coup in 2002, the country slipped into a civil war between north and south.

Cocoa prices weren't the only thing that triggered the war, but they were certainly a very significant factor in a country that was almost entirely dependent on cocoa exports until the 1990s. The German Federal Agency for Civic Education, together with the Bonn International Center for Conversion (BICC), put together a report on raw materials and conflicts, and the civil war in Côte d'Ivoire is included in it: 'There were also abuses in the cocoa sector's management that exacerbated social divides to the extent that they led to the 2002 rebellion.'[109]

But that's not all. Regardless of the civil war, the world carried on buying cocoa from Côte d'Ivoire; the chocolate show must go on. Both sides of the conflict used the proceeds to finance their war costs. The EU estimates that the government has used profits from the cocoa trade amounting to $45.7 million for military expenditure.[110]

Raw material conflicts – conflict raw materials

This makes cocoa a special case in the Ivorian civil war from the point of view of the politics of peace: it both caused and funded the conflict. It caused it because unfair distribution of cocoa profits further deepened existing social tensions and ultimately led to them erupting. And it funded it because both warring sides financed their arms purchases and their soldiers with the help of revenue from the cocoa trade.

In peace research, the different roles raw materials can have in conflicts are distinguished by the two terms 'raw material conflicts' and 'conflict raw materials'. A conflict raw material is a resource that's widely available in the war zone and that fetches high prices on the world market, therefore ensuring a constant supply of money and weapons. A typical example is diamonds; in Côte d'Ivoire it was cocoa. Conflict raw materials fund wars and sustain them for years, but they aren't usually the trigger for the conflict.

Raw material conflicts, on the other hand, have their origins in disputes over scarce resources, for example substances such as cocoa, oil or gold, or access to fertile land or fishing waters. The term refers to limited resources that two neighbouring countries or several groups within a country claim, and ultimately try to gain access to by force. If we look at it in terms of economics, this occurs when all the cooperative, peaceful sharing mechanisms that would normally regulate competition for scarce resources have failed. Economic competition then leads directly to war.[111]

The distinction between a raw material conflict and a conflict raw material is significant in helping us to find the right approaches to conflict resolution. If diamonds fund the war, but weren't its cause, putting a halt to the trade in 'blood diamonds' might help to contain the war, because it can curb the supply of money and weapons. The actual conflict is far from being resolved, though.

Often, however, competition for raw materials is actually the cause of violent conflicts. This is shown by the figures in the Conflict Barometer, published annually by the Heidelberg Institute for International Conflict Research (HIIK) and an important reference for the analysis of wars and conflicts worldwide. The 2022 Conflict Barometer records a total of 216 violent conflicts worldwide. In just under a third (70) of them, scarce resources were a factor as a cause of conflict, but were almost always linked with other causes as well.[112]

As a result, competition for raw materials is often a significant co-factor in the onset of wars because it can exacerbate existing inequalities or conflicts – as in the example of cocoa in Côte d'Ivoire. The good news is that if a significant cause of a conflict is in our hands, in our economic system, in food speculation or in our thirst for certain raw materials, potential solutions are also in our hands.

Blood diamonds

The same is also true of conflict raw materials. The most famous example of this is what were known as 'blood diamonds', which even made it to Hollywood. The 2006 film *Blood Diamonds* is still worth watching today because it highlighted the brutal link between the arms trade and the funding of wars with diamonds. This subject also features in Donna Leon's crime novels and the James Bond films, and that's a good thing.

The debate over blood diamonds – or conflict diamonds, as they are more formally known – began in the 1990s, when it became clear that the wars in Sierra Leone, Liberia and Angola were largely financed by diamond sales. The competition for diamonds wasn't a cause of the war in any of these countries. The precious stones only played a later role as the conflicts dragged on. The civil war in Sierra Leone, for example, began in 1991, but it wasn't until 1994 that the rebels occupied the diamond fields so they could carry on funding the war.

It was even more obvious in Angola. The civil war there began in the 1970s; a rebel organisation by the name of UNITA, supported by the US and South Africa, fought against the central government, which sided with the Eastern Bloc during the Cold War. It was only when international interest in the war waned with the end of the Cold War that diamonds came into play. According to calculations by the aid and human rights organisation Medico International, UNITA made around US$3.7 billion from diamonds between 1992 and 1998, which financed the continuation of the war.[113] Here, too, the beginning of the war had nothing to do with diamonds, but they featured much more heavily in its perpetuation later. Medico International used a haunting sentence about it: 'It is more profitable to exploit a war than to win it.'[114]

There are also instances where conflict raw materials take on a life of their own and become the main reason for ever-increasing violence: namely when the warring parties fight for the territories where the conflict raw materials are. This also makes it more difficult to find peaceful solutions. In Colombia, for example, the peace agreement – which was in fact a great success – is now under pressure again because various armed groups are trying to take control of the profitable coca-growing areas by force.

As long as your own funding is secured, your will to negotiate peace will always be half-hearted. This is why there have been repeated attempts in the past to curb the trade in conflict raw materials and drain the financial basis of bloody civil wars. Back in 1998, the UN Security Council approved a ban on the trade of the Angolan UNITA rebels' diamonds. In 2003, the Kimberley Process came into force, an agreement by the countries producing and buying the most diamonds worldwide on a certification system to stop the trade in blood diamonds. The members of the Kimberley Process now represent over 99 per cent of the world's diamond trade. Even though this process has certainly helped to make the trade in blood diamonds more difficult, there is also mass criticism of the system. Some of the NGOs originally involved have since withdrawn from the process because the controls have too many loopholes to be able to rule out forged certificates of origin.

Another conflict raw material also gained a certain prominence in the noughties because we hold it to our ears on a daily basis: coltan. This ore contains important metals that are mainly used in the electronics industry, especially in mobile phone production. A large share of the coltan mined worldwide comes from Africa, especially from the Democratic Republic of Congo, where for years the raw material was used to fund the civil war there. In this case, too, there was public pressure on the industrial sector to stop using coltan from civil war zones. In the US and other countries, legal requirements were soon in place for manufacturers to guarantee a clean origin for their coltan.

Support in monitoring these requirements came from the sciences: the German Federal Institute for Geosciences managed to develop a physical, chemical proof of origin for coltan, a 'fingerprint' that can be used to unequivocally determine the origin of every sample of coltan.[115] It's a great tool for putting a halt to unscrupulous smugglers and for ensuring our mobile phones don't help fund the bloody civil wars in Africa. That's a good first step, but an equally important second step would be improving mining conditions. As with cocoa, there is also a great potential for conflict in coltan: wages are far too low and working conditions in the mines are appalling.

Pirates and land grabbers

Let's go back to the raw material conflicts, or resource conflicts. We're probably all aware of oil's potential for conflict; plenty of peace demonstrations in Germany have had the slogan 'No blood for oil', in view of the many wars in the Middle East. But oil and cocoa are not alone: resource conflicts are so diverse and they affect almost every vital resource – there could be a whole book about them. Here are just two brief examples to show the many ways in which global economic interdependencies in a resource's countries of origin can lead to violence.

Let's start with illegal fishing. Worldwide, the seas are severely depleted from fishing. To protect fish stocks and to be able to catch fish in the future, there are now strict rules worldwide over who is allowed to catch how much fish and where. The practice of catching more – or fishing without a licence – is known as *illegal, unreported and unregulated (IUU) fishing*. But it occurs on an industrial scale. Off the coasts of Africa and Latin America, huge fishing trawlers from Europe or China cruise and poach practically everything from under the noses of the poor local fishing communities with their small boats. This is not only a big problem for the environment: it can also be the cause of war. Local fishing communities then have to look for other sources of income. And for someone who has always earned a living on the water and in a boat, it's not that far-fetched to think about turning to piracy, in view of a lack of legal alternatives. Rather than IUU fishing, they're making armed raids on other ships to hijack them and extort a high ransom.

This is exactly what happened in Somalia. In the noughties, raids on container ships on their way to the Suez Canal became a real problem. Even the German Navy was sent into action with warships ('Operation Atalanta') to secure the transport routes with military force. There are clear indications that piracy in the Horn of Africa has come into existence mainly because of IUU fishing by large international trawlers. The small fishing communities lost their previous law-abiding livelihood and switched to piracy in desperation. I hope I'm not justifying or romanticising piracy here – it's got nothing to do with Captain Jack Sparrow; it's a brutal business.

But we need to ask why governments only take action when container ships are threatened. There are scarcely any serious measures to counter international IUU fishing, which is carried out by European giant trawlers, among others, wreaking havoc worldwide and endangering the livelihoods of poor fishing families – and in the process, peace – in remote places all over the world. It would probably have helped to secure the shipping routes through the Suez Canal much more if all the money that went into Operation Atalanta had gone into combating IUU fishing in the years running up to it.

There's plenty that could be done about IUU fishing, if the political will existed. There are a wide variety of research projects working to detect and convict IUU fishers using scientific methods. There's one I particularly liked, published in the renowned *Proceedings of the National Academy of Sciences*: in 2020 a French research group set out a method to detect unregistered fishing trawlers in the expanses of the oceans – with the help of albatrosses.[116] The idea is as simple as it is ingenious. Albatrosses are really large birds that travel long distances over the sea, constantly in search of tasty fish. When they come across a fishing boat at work, they often spend a long time hovering over it, as there's usually something in it for them. The research group equipped albatrosses with small transmitters and used their flight paths to identify in real time fishing boats that couldn't be located electronically because they had switched off their detection signals – a clear indication that they were out at sea illegally.

There are ample ways to effectively combat IUU fishing and eliminate a potential cause of violent conflicts. Peace hasn't reigned in Somalia for a long time, as there are many divisions on land too. But the dispute over the resource of fish off the Somalia coast wouldn't have had to escalate into massive military violence if our governments here in Europe had cracked down more strictly on illegal fishing.

The second example of a resource conflict is related to 'land grabbing', the appropriation of land by international companies. A particularly dramatic example occurred in Madagascar in 2008 – and led to the collapse of the government after a series of violent protests. The South Korean company Daewoo Logistics wanted access to over a million hectares of land in Madagascar to grow corn and palm oil for the South Korean market. Daewoo was apparently going to take over the land for 99 years without paying a single cent of rent, only creating a few jobs in return. When the deal became well known through an article in the *Financial Times* – the government had kept it secret until then – there were immediate protests in Madagascar. The conflict escalated quickly, and there were several very violent demonstrations in which over a hundred people died.[117] Only when the president left the country and his successor put a halt to the deal did the situation calm down again. Land grabbing is still occurring in many regions of the world, and has great potential to escalate existing conflicts or spark new ones, as land is always related to many people's direct livelihoods, their homes and their food.

From trade wars to unpeaceful trade

In colonial times, the slogan 'War starts here' still had a very direct meaning, when heavily armed European countries invaded other areas, enslaved people and committed genocides, or used coercive power to enforce certain trade rights. Back then, trade wars weren't fought with punitive tariffs and predatory prices, but with cannons and rifles. A classic example of this is the Opium Wars that Britain waged against China in the mid-nineteenth century. The cause was quite trivial: a great imbalance in trade between the two countries. The British bought vast quantities of tea, silk and porcelain from China, but had scarcely any goods to offer in return that anyone could have bought in China. To compensate for the huge trade deficit, Britain blithely entered the opium trade.

The drug was produced in India and illegally sold to China, where addiction soon became a massive social problem. The Emperor of China tried to put an end to it, and confiscated entire shiploads of opium. The British responded with war, and ultimately China had to agree to a deeply unjust peace treaty that granted the Europeans extensive trade rights in China. It was a trade war waged with warships and cannons, and it would bring a huge empire to its knees economically for many decades.

But genuine, bloody trade wars were far from over. Until the 1950s, arms were repeatedly taken up to enforce economic interests by force. When the democratically elected government of Guatemala approved a land reform in 1952, it met with fierce resistance from a US banana concern, the United Fruit Company. The government wanted the company to give up part of its land, in exchange for compensation, of course. The discussion was only ever about land that was completely undeveloped. Nevertheless, the company was outraged and mobilised Washington. With the CIA's help, a coup was staged in Guatemala in 1954, and the democratic government was replaced by a military dictatorship. It all goes to show that war can even break out over bananas. The consequences were horrendous; a bloody civil war raged in Guatemala until 1966, and to this day the country has still not recovered from it – and all because a banana company wasn't willing to sell land it wasn't using to the government. (By the way, nowadays the United Fruit Company is known as Chiquita.)

As we've seen with chocolate, diamonds and fishing, unjust economic relationships in the world can still lead to very real wars or violent conflicts. That's why it's often said that economic issues are issues of national security as well – and why, in turn, the trade routes through the Suez Canal are sometimes safeguarded by German warships, or why France's access to uranium in Niger is protected by soldiers. But if economic issues are deciding factors for a war's outcome, they can also bring war about. Here in Europe we need an economic policy that engenders peace, rather than wars, in the world. The former UN Special Rapporteur Jean Ziegler once wrote about development assistance: 'It isn't about giving more to the people of the Third World, but about stealing less from them.'[118]

Some measures have already come into force. The German 2023 Supply Chain Act is a start and ensures companies prevent human rights violations – and as a result, potential causes of war – in manufacturing countries. In the case of cocoa, there will soon be traceability, right down to the individual farm. But there's still a lot to do, from banning food speculation to ending unfair trade agreements. Peace work also means taking on the companies that fuel wars elsewhere in the world.

13

DISARMAMENT FROM ABOVE AND FROM BELOW

In the corridors of the UN headquarters in New York there are works of art from all over the world that various countries have given to the UN: a life-sized golden dodo from Mauritius, steel drums from the Caribbean, the finest tapestries from Iran. They are as diverse as the world itself: some ostentatious and glitzy, some playfully kitsch, and often symbols of peace and disarmament. A section of the Berlin Wall is in the garden there too. And there's a pistol. The pistol says everything there is to say about war and peace, security and disarmament.

This pistol with a knot in its barrel is the complete antithesis of the idea that safety comes from the barrel of a gun, and that peace is only possible if you arm yourself to the hilt. This idea is cleverly packaged in worn-out cliches such as 'If you want peace, prepare for war', often quoted in Latin, which it makes it sound even more grand. The former East German version of the slogan was 'Peace must be armed.' No, it doesn't have to be. Security isn't something we need to use against each other; it works much better when we use it together, in a cooperative security policy, as we know from the early 1970s policy of détente.

Egon Bahr – the master of détente

There's a theme that seems to be recurring throughout this book: the fact that conflicts aren't a problem in themselves.

There are always conflicts, everywhere. It just depends on how you solve them: together or against each other? Peacefully or violently? If you have 100 nuclear bombs, do I build 200? Or do we disarm together in our common interest, with mutual agreement and governance?

This isn't a utopia: it was once a reality, during the Cold War's heyday. Back then, two blocs were irreconcilably opposed to each other, and each questioned the other ideology's right to exist. They were arch enemies, in rhetoric and with every fibre of their social systems. And yet they managed to reach mutual agreements on security issues, conclude major disarmament treaties, and launch the Conference on Security and Cooperation in Europe (CSCE). How was that possible?

It began with the Cuban Missile Crisis in 1962, when the world was closer than ever to the brink of an earth-shattering nuclear war. This was followed by the sober realisation that atomic bombs might not be a guarantee of peace after all and that mutual discussion could create much more security. Back in 1963, the first step towards rapprochement was an agreement to put a halt to certain nuclear tests, and many other disarmament treaties followed. It was the start of what would later be called a policy of détente or cooperative security, as an alternative to armament and war.

The secret at the heart of cooperative security lies in thinking about the other side's security interests, and in responding to them: if the other side feels threatened, it arms itself, and so cooperation ends. It is important to note that this sense of security cannot be objectified. Even if I don't understand a security concern from the other side and think it's completely inappropriate, if one side feels threatened, I have to take it seriously: only if both sides feel safe can they refrain from further armament.

I was once able to learn how this can work in concrete terms from Egon Bahr personally. His name is probably linked to the détente policy of the seventies more than anyone else's in Germany. In 1963, he coined the term 'change through rapprochement' and, as the right-hand man of the foreign minister, and later chancellor, Willy Brandt, he was the mastermind and architect of the détente policy. Almost exactly fifty years later, I met him in person, and to this day I'm grateful for that opportunity: Egon Bahr was not only very clever and probably the most experienced foreign policy expert of his time, he was also a really nice person, and a very relaxed one, in line with his policy. Back then, we were cautiously meeting under the radar, with the task of gauging for our parties whether and to what extent cooperation between the Left Party and the SPD (the German Social Democratic Party) might be possible when it came to foreign policy. We argued a lot, and we always had fun while we were at it. One day he told me an anecdote that wonderfully illustrates the essence of cooperative security.

In the early 1970s, the armed forces were meant to finally reach their target strength of 500,000 men (at that time it was still just men). The Soviet Union felt threatened by this, while NATO would have felt unprotected with a smaller defence force. A solution was essential to reconcile each side's security concerns. Egon Bahr said he asked his defence minister, Georg Leber, what could be done. After a while, he came back with two suggestions: the armed forces could dismantle their field hospitals and their bridge-building companies. After all, you can defend your territory without laying bridges, which are mainly needed for fighting on foreign territory. Egon Bahr then called the Soviet foreign minister at the time, Andrei Gromyko, and presented him with the proposal. He just said one thing (and at this point in the story Egon Bahr took on a very deep, gravelly voice): 'I'll have to ask my generals about that.' Two weeks later, the return call came: 'That's fine, we can go with that.'

I don't know if the anecdote really played out exactly like that, but Egon Bahr certainly had a wonderful way of telling it, and it illustrates two things at the core of cooperative security. First, if your opposite number feels threatened, take it seriously and find a solution. The alternative would have been for the Soviet Union to respond to German armed forces expansion by arming itself more, and the spiral would have started again.

Second, it's a nice example of an armament concept that's known as 'structural non-aggression capability'. Yes, there might well be an army that's armed to the hilt and that can defend itself, but it's designed in a way that it's scarcely able to attack another country. No bridge-building companies, no fear of attack. From a pacifist point of view, structural non-aggression capability isn't ideal, as it's still based on a logic of weapons and armament. However, it can be a valuable intermediate step in reducing tensions at times when complete disarmament isn't yet a possibility. It's not quite a knot in the barrel of a pistol, but it's getting there.

Disarming by getting rid of what's no longer needed

It is worth taking a closer look at the steps taken to disarm after the shock of the Cuban Missile Crisis, because they highlight the unpleasant basic principles we'll have to deal with in disarmament initiatives in the future. In essence, the weapons being limited or eliminated were ones that were no longer needed, that could be replaced by new weapons or that were no longer appropriate for the concepts of war prevailing at the time. A good example of this is the 1972 Biological Weapons Convention, which approved a complete ban on the production and stockpiling of biological weapons. In Chapter 7, on the biologist Matthew Meselson, we looked in detail at the power and political considerations at the time, such as how US President Nixon unilaterally declared an abandonment of biological weapons. The reason was simply that in an age of nuclear deterrence, they were of little use to the US. The global ban on biological weapons was a smart move: a potential threat to the US was eliminated without significantly restricting its own forces' combat capabilities. In this way, and only in this way, biological disarmament could be set in motion: by getting rid of what was no longer needed.

That might sound sobering, but it's still a great step forward. Without the Biological Weapons Convention, biological weapons would probably be a gruesome everyday occurrence in today's wars, and no one would be safe from manufactured pathogens. A global ban is a good thing, regardless of how calculating the US's political and power-related thinking was at the time.

The realisation that disarmament usually only involves weapons that are no longer needed doesn't have to be debilitating. On the contrary: we can use it to form good strategies for steps towards disarmament in the future. After all, what the military still needs and what it doesn't often depends on the particular conditions in question, and these can change. A good example of how an agreement changed conditions so that further disarmament could become possible is the ABM Treaty of the early 1970s: the Anti-Ballistic Missile Treaty.

In the 1960s, nuclear disarmament was discussed worldwide. There was deep shock over the two atomic bombings of Hiroshima and Nagasaki, and many scientists involved in the bomb's construction, such as Robert Oppenheimer, campaigned for a ban on all nuclear weapons. However, the nuclear powers, above all the US and the Soviet Union, didn't want to be deprived of this mighty weapon and armed themselves against each other as if they were obsessed. Both sides developed new defensive missiles that could intercept approaching nuclear missiles. It was clear to both of them that it was precisely those defence systems that had opened the door to a limitless arms race: if you build ten defence systems, I'll build 100 nuclear weapons; if you build 100 nuclear weapons, I'll build 1,000 defence systems; it was an endless spiral, with an ever-increasing risk of error and incredibly high costs. Neither side wanted this situation, so in the ABM Treaty in 1972 they agreed that each side was only allowed to install two of these defence systems.[119] And as soon as that was decided, the number of nuclear missiles could also be reduced again. Without the ABM Treaty, subsequent agreements limiting nuclear weapons would not have been possible. It was a good blueprint for future disarmament initiatives: changing the conditions by limiting armament so that other limitations suddenly become possible.

Disarming by getting rid of what you don't have yourself

Another potential path to disarmament is only allowing weapons for those countries that already have them – and to ban them for all the others. It sounds absurd: who would ever sign up to such a bad deal? But it has in fact happened, and with nuclear weapons, of all things. To understand, we have to go way back to the 1960s. There was a great desire for nuclear disarmament worldwide, but at the same time the five nuclear weapon states – the US, USSR, China, Britain and France – didn't want to be deprived of this weapon under any circumstances. For them, a total ban was unthinkable. Conversely, everyone wanted to avoid more and more countries getting the bomb, as well as the prospect of every conflict, no matter how small, potentially turning into a nuclear war.

Against this backdrop, the Non-Proliferation Treaty (NPT) was adopted, taking the various parties' interests into account in three ways: first, the five nuclear powers committed themselves to the long-term goal of nuclear disarmament; second, all other countries that signed the treaty renounced nuclear armament; third, all countries were promised international cooperation with the peaceful use of nuclear energy. It wasn't a result that we'd want these days, but in the thinking prevalent in the 1960s, nuclear power was still considered a true saviour. And an agreement covering more wasn't feasible at that time; anyone who wanted effective monitoring of nuclear weapons had to agree to the concept of an exclusive club of the five nuclear powers. The threat of nuclear war was far from written off, but the NPT managed to keep the number of nuclear powers really low – today we have nine; in addition to the five previous ones, India, Pakistan, Israel and North Korea now also have nuclear arms, and are all nations that either didn't join the NPT in the first place or eventually withdrew from it.

Disarming by getting rid of what doesn't yet exist

In principle, the NPT is based on countries renouncing a weapon they don't yet have. This can also be applied to future technologies. A ban on weapons that we don't yet have the technology to produce is easier to enforce: once a country has a certain weapon system and considers it militarily valuable, the ban won't stand, as we've seen earlier. It was no different when they started looking at nuclear disarmament. The initial agreement dealt with a ban on nuclear weapons in space with the 1967 Outer Space Treaty. Back then, the first satellites were already being used in space, and there were intercontinental missiles, but the idea of permanently stationing nuclear missiles in space or even building military bases on the moon was technically unimaginable. A ban was therefore easy for the US and the USSR to agree to at the time.

This experience later gave rise to the concept of preventive arms control, which looks at new technologies on the basis of current armament dynamics and identifies potential future weapons systems that are preventable.[120] A current example of this is fully autonomous weapons: weapon systems that decide between life and death completely independently. If they classify a person as a potential danger or an opponent on the basis of their programming, they shoot – without a human being making the decision. If there's no longer a person in the loop, it's classed technically as a 'lethal autonomous weapon system'.

There's also a much clearer term for these kinds of systems: killer robots.

Systems of this kind aren't available yet – but they are already raising major ethical questions. If the decision over life and death is left to a machine, it's difficult to predict when this machine will turn against someone, and who that someone might be. It's so close to science fiction scenarios where robots get out of control and turn against humanity that there have been some serious attempts to outlaw fully autonomous weapons internationally. Negotiations to ban autonomous weapons have been going on at the UN in Geneva for about ten years now, and the German government has also campaigned for a ban. The talks are still ongoing, but they've clearly missed the ideal moment for it. Technical possibilities have developed to such an extent in the meantime that military powers are showing great interest in these weapons – once again primarily the US and Russia, neither of which wants an international agreement, but at most some kind of voluntary commitment. In hindsight, we can see that in 2014 it was a good, forward-looking move to strive for a treaty of this kind, but as with all other weapons systems, it's also true that if a military power believes it needs, or has its sights on, certain weapons, disarmament will be very difficult to achieve.

This also links closely to drones. For many years there have been calls for a global ban on armed drones, in view of the countless lethal drone attacks by the US in many countries around the world. A ban would be crucial: combat drones have the effect of neutralising war, as attacks become risk-free for the perpetrators. If you let machines do the fighting for you, you'll be quicker to resort to violence and kill people in other places. It's only a tiny step from drones to fully autonomous weapons, even if it's still a human at a screen making the final decision about a deadly drone attack and pressing the button.

However, I fear that any hope for an agreement controlling drones is in vain, as hardly any weapons are as coveted as drones are by the military right now. In the Ukraine war, it's particularly clear: we can see how small, inexpensive drones have become the most important weapon in this terrible war of attrition. In this situation, no country in the world will agree to do without a weapons system like this in the future. It's a sobering, painful realisation, but unfortunately that's the way it is.

Disarmament from below – here's how it can work

From all these experiences, one thing's becoming clear: if we leave disarmament to governments, the outlook isn't good. They're not interested in having their military means of power taken away from them. If we seriously want to disarm, then we, as civil society, have to take it into our own hands, just like with the landmines, the Arms Trade Treaty, the Treaty on the Prohibition of Nuclear Weapons – all wonderful examples of how disarmament from below can be a complete success.

Until the end of the Cold War, disarmament was primarily a matter between Moscow and Washington. In practically every country, security policy was the sole domain of state authority, and civil society had scarcely anything to do with it. For a long time, international disarmament negotiations weren't open to civil organisations. I still remember sitting alone in the corridors of the UN building in Geneva outside the biological weapons negotiations, which were going on behind closed doors – while in the room opposite, hundreds of NGOs were taking part in environmental negotiations.

And then the landmine campaign happened: a disarmament process that was largely initiated by civil society. The initiative put governments under so much public pressure that ultimately, they were forced to make security policy concessions in the form of a ban on landmines. How could that have happened? I talked about this at length with Anne Jung, who has been working for Medico International in Frankfurt for 25 years. It's one of the most interesting human rights organisations in Germany, combining concrete humanitarian aid in the field with political work, along the lines of the principle that help alone is not enough: you have to change the circumstances.

This was also the case with landmines. In countries such as Angola and Cambodia, Medico regularly witnessed the horrific consequences of mines. Even if war was long over, the mines were still lying hidden in fields and on paths, an ever-present mortal danger. Years later, the poorest of the poor were still suffering from the consequences, agriculture was restricted, access routes were disrupted and deaths and injuries occurred again and again. It was clear that a long-term solution to the problem was needed. And so Medico initiated a global campaign for a ban on landmines, together with several other organisations in the US and from the southern hemisphere.[121]

Right from the outset, they went global – and aimed big. Other organisations were persuaded to join in, offices were set up in Germany and worldwide, and then, step by step, politicians were persuaded to take up the cause. The focus was always on the humanitarian aspect: the many deaths, the civilian population's suffering, the fact that landmines meant the war was never actually over. Soon the cultural sector also found out about the issue: it reached TV screens and the media, and in Angola, Princess Diana stood in the middle of a minefield wearing a flak jacket – an iconic image. Anne Jung remembers that years later in Angola she was always being asked about it; everyone had a friend of a friend who had seen the princess back then. The campaign touched hearts around the world and paved the way for a political solution.

In politics, things usually only happen when the powers that be are afraid that doing nothing will ruin their election results. If people on the streets don't want landmines any more, they'll say so at the ballot box. After pressure from civil society in many countries, over a hundred countries finally approved a global ban on anti-personnel mines in 1997. Even though the main obstructors – the US, Russia and China – haven't signed the agreement, it's working. At some point, the moment came when more mines were cleared than were being laid. Since then, a powerful global norm against landmines has been established – a moral and political ostracism that's had such a big effect that even the US now largely adheres to the agreement.

The huge success of the landmine campaign, which was awarded the Nobel Peace Prize in 1997, has been the inspiration and impetus for other disarmament campaigns coming from below, especially the Treaty on the Prohibition of Nuclear Weapons, which came into force in 2021, not to be confused with the old Non-Proliferation Treaty. In actual fact, there are currently two international treaties on nuclear weapons: the old NPT of 1969, which decrees that there can be an exclusive club of five nuclear powers and which only prohibits nuclear weapons for all other nations, and now the new treaty, which bans all nuclear weapons without exception. Of course, the nuclear powers haven't signed it; neither are the NATO countries on board. Nevertheless, it cannot be valued highly enough, as it's renewed and reinforced the old norm against nuclear weapons. This was urgently needed, because many countries were increasingly questioning the NPT after the five nuclear powers had consistently refused to disarm for decades, even though this was one of the NPT's key commitments. In this case, too, a small NGO was needed to provide the impetus. ICAN (International Campaign to Abolish Nuclear Weapons) was founded as an umbrella organisation, and was awarded the Nobel Peace Prize in 2017.

The future of disarmament

Disarmament is, and will remain, a very important cornerstone for a more peaceful world, and an initial step towards a world without arms. Every weapon that's scrapped or that isn't produced in the first place is one less weapon that can be used for death and destruction. The fewer arms in circulation, the sooner wars reach their limits, and the more space there is for civil solutions. At the moment, we can't expect much from state authorities in terms of disarmament. On the contrary: more and more treaties are being revoked, and almost all the disarmament architecture from the second half of the last century is collapsing right before our eyes.

There is the sacrosanct NATO guideline for all member states to commit two per cent of their GDP to defence spending, plus Germany has set up a special fund of €100 billion for the armed forces, and many other European countries have approved similarly gargantuan armament spending. We are at the beginning of a new arms race of unimagined dimensions.

Right now, the Russia–Ukraine war dominates our consciousness. Many people wonder whether more European forces might not be the safer way in view of Russian aggression. This is understandable, but in my view it will lead to a dead end in the long term, as one thing is certain: whatever the outcome of the war in Ukraine, whatever happens in the next few decades, if we look at the map of the world in 50 years' time, Russia will still be our neighbour. There are only two possibilities: either we live in permanent confrontation with each other, or we move towards a peaceful coexistence. (I can't imagine coexistence at the moment, but nothing in this world can be ruled out.) Permanent confrontation means a limitless arms race, isolation and the constant threat of violent escalation – no one (except the arms industry) would want that in the long run.

The idea behind a huge amount of armaments is the hope that money will buy security. It's a big mistake, in my opinion. Money can buy weapons, but not security. In sections of Israeli society, 7 October 2023 is also seen as proof that security doesn't come from the barrel of a gun. The Israeli army is the most experienced, best equipped and most highly trained in the entire region – and yet it was unable to prevent the atrocities of 7 October. There was no chance against a terrorist threat, no matter how many tanks were lined up. If you only think in military terms, you'll never be able to guarantee genuine security.

The alternative would be a cooperative security system, as we had in the Cold War. That sounds unimaginable today, but it was reality before – and we weren't friends, even at that point. For there to be any chance of this, we should take care not to set the course in the wrong direction now. The €100 billion package and NATO's two per cent target, for example, are precisely the wrong decisions, because they're taking us down the path to the arms race started by Russia. Russia is expected to have the largest increase in military spending worldwide in 2024. This, and the attack on Ukraine, naturally create fear and uncertainty, which is only understandable.

However, the bare figures show a different picture: NATO already spends many times more on defence than Russia. Even if we take Russia's lesser purchasing power into account, the Russian military budget isn't even half as great as the European NATO countries' – and the US with its huge military budget isn't even included in that figure.[122] If there are calls for more money to be spent on weapons in Western European countries now, the first question should be 'What for?' Why wouldn't a defence budget twice as big as Russia's be enough? There should also be discussion of the horrendous costs of foreign missions and the question of what should take priority: national defence or military excursions to the other side of the world? Before constantly calling for more money, the money already allocated needs to be spent sensibly first – and we're allowed to cast doubt on that.

But now, down to specifics: What about Ukraine and the Middle East?

The many experiences from previous peace processes we've looked at in this book can offer hope for a more peaceful future. They can show us how conflicts were able to be contained, and how wars were able to be prevented or ended more quickly. But what does this mean for the wars going on right now? You might have picked up this book because you were affected by the daily horror in Ukraine or in Israel and Palestine and wanted to find out more about it. I'm going to look at the question of how all these experiences could bring us closer to peace in the here and now, with the two major wars so much on our minds at the moment.

14

Peace for Ukraine?

Back in the introduction, I said this book wouldn't be a detailed master plan for ending the Russian war of aggression on Ukraine: that simply doesn't exist. There are, though, many small steps other countries could take to promote peace in Ukraine. We've seen some of them in this book. They could play a significant role in Ukraine.

It starts with putting thinking about peaceful solutions back on the agenda in the first place. For over two years now, there's been almost nothing but constant argument in Europe over the grade and number of weapons that should be supplied to Ukraine. Questions about diplomacy and negotiations were at best ridiculed, and often met with abuse and forced out of the debate. If we had heard the word 'negotiations' at least a tenth of the times the Taurus gun brand has been mentioned in recent months, we would have made plenty of progress by now.

No one has a simple answer

Since the Russian attack on Ukraine began, I've been taking part in a lot of discussion events throughout Germany. No matter where I've been, in the East or in the West, with young people or old, one thing has always quickly become clear: there's uncertainty everywhere. Because there are no simple answers. Raul Zelik summed it up neatly in an article for the newspaper *Freitag* in spring 2023: 'All the "realpolitik" solutions are catastrophic. If Russia conquers Ukraine militarily, it is an invitation to every imperialist project to attack neighbouring countries. If, on the other hand, NATO supplies state-of-the-art weapons to prevent the collapse of Ukraine, it will perpetuate a war of attrition, at the end of which hundreds of thousands, at worst billions, of people will be dead.'[123]

Let's start with his second point: more weapons always mean an intensification of war. Yes, Russia's the aggressor, and Ukraine's defending itself, and we side entirely with the people of Ukraine. But it's also true that a longer war leads to more death, displacement and suffering. From a military logic, wars only end when all sides are tired of the war, and that takes years. If we think back to Afghanistan in 1979, the Soviet Union marched in with its entire military machine. The West then offered support to various Afghan militias with weapons to stop the invasion. The resistance was a success, but at what cost? It took ten long years for the Soviet Union to withdraw, and even after that the war did not stop. There has been uninterrupted war in Afghanistan ever since 1979. In other words, if you're looking for a *quick* path to peace, you shouldn't play the military card.

The first point made by Raul Zelik is just as important: if, as a result of this aggression, Russia can annex large parts of Ukraine without the rest of the world reacting, many people's suffering in Ukraine will be drawn out and international law – to which the people of Ukraine have a right – will be undermined. We've already argued this point when it came to the 2003 US aggression in Iraq, and on many other occasions: if we don't defend international law, it's an invitation to all the major countries of the world to invade their smaller neighbours. It's essential to prevent this, just as much as a long-lasting war.

So, is there no hope from the outset? Are all realpolitik solutions catastrophic? As the debate can sometimes be so poisonous, I'd just like to make one thing clear: people who speak out in favour of supplying arms to Ukraine aren't actually warmongers. Personally, I don't agree with supplying arms, but I can understand the urge many people have: we can't turn our backs on the Ukrainians while they're fighting for their lives right now. For the people who are currently defending their homes in Zaporizhzhia, a bazooka is better than no bazooka. It's hard to say no to that. But to agree to it, without reservation and without an alternative, isn't right either.

Anyone who accepts this 'either/or' question has already lost. We must never get caught up in the perceived dichotomy of violence or inaction. The question must always remain: what civil alternatives are there? If there isn't a *good* realpolitik course of action, maybe there's one that's *less bad*? As I said, I'm not a radical pacifist, but I do stand up for prioritising a civil approach – always trying non-military solutions first – as I described in the chapter on supplying arms, with the example of weapons for Kurdistan.

Wasted opportunities

There were, and are, opportunities for civil solutions for Ukraine, too. Unfortunately, some have been carelessly wasted, but they were there. In the first chapter of this book, the example of Syria showed us that in a war, what's missing is almost always a 'bigger person', someone prepared to give in. If people think only in terms of war logic, they'll think of victory when there's a military advantage, rather than negotiations. This was also the case in Ukraine in the autumn of 2022, when a window might have been open for negotiations. Ukraine had managed to stop the Russian advance: the strategically important city of Kherson was liberated and the Russian forces were forced to retreat to the Dnieper's eastern banks. For the first time in the war, there was momentum on the Ukrainian side.

In this situation, then US Chairman of the Joint Chiefs of Staff Mark Milley made an almost unprecedented recommendation: 'You want to negotiate at a time when you're at strength and your opponent is at weakness.'[124] He also very clearly warned: 'So when there's an opportunity to negotiate, when peace can be achieved, seize it, seize the moment.'[125] This suggestion unfortunately couldn't come to fruition because the military dynamics outweighed everything else at the time, and Ukraine believed it was on the road to victory. That was a mistake.

Another chance was wasted: in the chapter on sanctions, we saw that economic measures can only be effective if they are introduced quickly and comprehensively. The Kremlin had learned one thing from the experience in 2014 after the annexation of Crimea: the EU is very reluctant to impose economic sanctions and avoids anything that could damage its own economy whenever possible. Therefore, in February 2022, the Russian government could be fairly certain that the all-important money from oil would continue to flow – Moscow probably calculated that the EU would never shoot itself in the foot. And they were right. The oil embargo only took effect over a year later, and Russia made more money than ever before from oil during the first year of the war, as a result of the enormous price hike on the world market. The government was able to fund its attack on Ukraine with their European oil roubles. The opportunity to influence the war early on through sanctions was wasted. Russia had all the time in the world to build up a tanker fleet so it could carry on selling oil on the world market even after the EU embargo.

The argument that an oil embargo would have hit Germany harder than Russia doesn't stand up. In the end, it's a question of money, and there clearly was enough money. Immediately after the Russian aggression, the German government approved a €100 billion package for armament so it could counter Russia militarily. If there had been a €100 billion package for a transition to sustainable energy – and for capping energy prices for consumers – Russia could have been cut off and all the oil embargo's consequences could easily have been absorbed. It was a political decision that chose the military path over the civil.

Prepare for negotiations to make them a possibility

These opportunities were wasted, but others are still open to us now. Even today, I can still see two civil approaches that haven't been pursued at all, or far too little: active diplomacy that is willing to incur the costs, and economic pressure on the Kremlin.

In Chapter 1, we saw that negotiations become more likely when they are prepared for, when there is a public, international discussion and a certain amount of pressure from various sides, as in Bosnia. The outside world needed to be 'roused from a state of shock', as the former head of the Munich Security Conference, Wolfgang Ischinger, put it.

The 'bigger player' principle has also played an important part in preparing for peace negotiations in the past. If we apply it to the Russia–Ukraine war, this would mean persuading China to influence Russia to move towards peace negotiations. 'Pressure' would be too strong a word here: the mutual dependencies between Russia and China are too great for that and Beijing would be unlikely to stab Moscow in the back.

But even the Chinese leadership sees this war as a big mistake and a threat to its own interests, and has publicly criticised it from the outset. The Konrad Adenauer Foundation office in Beijing summed it up as soon as the war began, saying that China had 'little to gain from the war, but much to lose'.[126] At the beginning of 2023, China presented a 12-point paper on the Russia–Ukraine war. It was neither a peace plan nor a roadmap for negotiations, but it did set out the People's Republic's basic position on the war. In essence, it contained a clear criticism of the Russian invasion of Ukraine. It would be good to see the paper as an offer to the West and use it accordingly: this is our view of things, and if you like, we could start a conversation on this basis. But China also made it clear that the Ukraine war is not very high on its list of priorities; it's seen in Beijing as more of a European problem.

In my view, it would have been a very good investment of political capital if Europe had taken China up on this offer.

Instead, it was either ignored or ridiculed over here. The great rivalry between the US and China is what lies behind this – a genuine world power conflict between the old superpower, the US, and the emerging superpower, China. In this conflict, the EU has recently very clearly and explicitly sided with the US. This is understandable from economic and geopolitical points of view, but this thinking leads directly to a new Cold War, with two superpowers and their respective partners irreconcilably opposed to each other. Neither the major crises of our time (above all the climate disaster) nor the Russian war of aggression can be tackled in this way.

A significant public upgrade of China's image on the international stage would have been essential to win over the Chinese leadership for active intervention. That may well be wrong, given the human rights violations in China, but we need to be clear that a quick path to peace negotiations is scarcely imaginable without China's help. To give the people of Ukraine a possibility of a faster return to peace, I would always advocate paying this political price.

I'm explicitly calling it a possibility here: no one can be certain that China taking a strong active role will genuinely lead to serious peace negotiations. I'm convinced that Vladimir Putin would definitely sit down at the table if Xi Jinping invited him: he's far too dependent on China to do anything else. Only an attempt can show us how seriously these negotiations might go and whether a just peace for Ukraine could ultimately be implemented. But it's definitely an opportunity for a faster peace agreement – and more so than simply focusing on supplying arms.

Nor will it suffice to just hold talks about potential peace negotiations behind the scenes. That certainly will have happened (or at least I hope so) when, for example, German Chancellor Olaf Scholz was in Beijing in the spring of 2024. Behind closed doors, viewpoints can be exchanged and common goals explored, but there's no momentum for negotiations. As happened in Bosnia or Northern Ireland, there needs to be a widespread public debate about peace solutions, and gentle but tangible pressure from a 'bigger player'.

Germany has to decide: does it want to keep close with the United States in the world power conflict or risk a public re-evaluation of China, if it might open a window of opportunity for peace? My moral compass is very clear here: the Chancellor could have taken a flight to Beijing for every battle tank supplied.

Making it possible to talk about diplomatic solutions

I'm often told that supplying arms and diplomacy aren't mutually exclusive, and that both are essential. That's true in theory, but the reality has been very different in the course of the first years of the Ukraine war. To this day, I'm stunned by how vehemently people pit diplomacy and supplying arms against each other. The arguments are almost always about battle tanks or Taurus cruise missiles, and practically never about potential ways to negotiate. In fact, only one of these is implemented, and the other's steered clear of.

History shows that most wars have ended through negotiation, and not with a military victory. So we should get the people who are so vehemently in favour of supplying fighter-bombers and Taurus missiles to answer the question of how we can bring about effective negotiations more quickly. In the past two years, though, we've seen an exclusivism come into the debate in Germany, making any conversation about diplomacy impossible.

I'd like to see a little more humility on all sides. The absolute certainty with which supplying arms is seen as the only way to a just peace is misguided. If people think that Kyiv would have fallen after just a few days if arms hadn't been sent, they're simply wrong. When the Russian columns were bogged down before Kyiv and beaten into retreat by Ukraine, only a few days had passed since the war had begun, and the debate about supplying arms was only just starting. On the other hand, it is true – and the pacifist side must face this fact, too – that Russia would be very likely to have control over larger sections of Ukraine by now if no weapons had been supplied. Weapons make a difference in war; it's undeniable. But whether they also make a difference for a just peace is a completely different question. It wouldn't be the first time in history that parts of a country occupied by the enemy were liberated again at the negotiating table. For example, after the Camp David negotiations in 1979, Israel returned occupied Sinai to Egypt.

Only if diplomacy becomes a genuine option again can future opportunities be put to good use, even if it might not look like it at the moment: if there is military momentum from the Ukrainian side again, as there was in autumn 2022, there should be plenty of Mark Milleys trying to open the door to negotiations.

Security guarantees

Looking at Ukraine, I'm deliberately talking about a *just* peace. A peace with Russia in control of large parts of Ukrainian territory is not a just peace. It cannot be a pacifist stance to say that the Kremlin should be given what it wants for the sake of peace, as nothing would then stop Russia from invading other neighbouring countries – it would mean even more war instead of peace. This is why the goal must be a just peace, a peace where the aggressor doesn't win and a peace that the people of Ukraine can agree to by a large majority.

It would include security guarantees, which must be very specific and very effective so that Ukraine could agree to a solution; they won't trust contractual assurances from Russia at the moment, with good reason. Even after a peace agreement might be concluded, it will take many years before trust can slowly begin to build between the two countries again. It's impossible to speed this up with a few quick confidence-building measures in the course of negotiations.

Viable security guarantees from other states are scarcely likely – the NATO countries have repeatedly made it abundantly clear that they won't defend Ukraine with their own troops. Promising Ukraine that it can become a member of NATO later doesn't alter this fact: it will never happen in the middle of the war, if ever. An attempt by French President Macron to bring NATO ground troops into play was emphatically rejected by all the other NATO countries. So we need another solution that's more than just a piece of paper – a solution that can provide real security for Ukraine. Finding that will be one of the key problems in a Russian–Ukrainian peace agreement.

It requires dozens of creative ideas, which then go on to become so well defined as negotiations progress that both sides can see their security interests taken into account. Here's just one example. Experienced observers assume that a potential ceasefire line between Russia and Ukraine can only be policed by the UN. OSCE, for example, wouldn't be able to deal with such a mammoth task. But how could Russia be prevented from simply crossing the line again despite the presence of UN peacekeeping forces? One idea would be for some of the UN troops to come from China and countries allied with Russia. It's hard to imagine the Russian leadership giving an order to attack which would endanger the lives of Chinese soldiers; Russia is too dependent on China's loyalty. Whether China would be willing to take on the peacekeeping task, whether that would be enough for Ukraine, whether it would even accept Chinese troops on its own border and which other countries could provide a balance – these are all questions that would have to be clarified in open-ended negotiations. But one thing is certain: without robust mechanisms guaranteeing each side's security, neither of them will agree to a treaty.

Pressure on the Kremlin

Active diplomacy involving Russia's close allies is one thing. But that alone won't be enough to persuade the Kremlin to make concessions at a future negotiating table. Economic pressure is also important. One way to do this is through sanctions. We've missed the ideal time for oil sanctions, but other targeted sanctions still have the potential to change the cost-benefit calculation in Moscow. In the chapter on sanctions, I looked at the French economist Thomas Piketty's proposal to impose sanctions not only on the super-rich – the so-called oligarchs – in Russia, but also on the upper middle class, the heart of the Russian economy. This hasn't happened as yet.

A closer look at the EU's sanctions against Russia to date shows that they are full of loopholes. This is because many EU countries have done everything they can to keep their own valuable economic sectors exempt from the sanctions wherever possible. The Belgian diamond trade example we saw in Chapter 11 is just one of many. Other findings from sanctions research were also wantonly disregarded. For example, nothing has been clearly formulated about the conditions for lifting the sanctions against Russia. The EU's resolutions on the Russia sanctions don't even specify clear goals.

The concept of lifting sanctions can be taken another step further, by combining sanctions with incentive systems. Incentives needn't just refer to the lifting of sanctions, but more far-reaching proposals too. For example, there could be incentives for individuals on sanctions lists to act as whistleblowers reporting on their own regime. Politically, the idea of incentives is of course tricky, as they could also be seen as an indirect reward for aggression: I'm attacking my neighbour; what will you offer to make me stop? It's a very fine line between, on the one hand, using every possibility to end a conflict, and on the other, creating undesirable incentives for aggression.

Learning from history

The fact that the war has quickly taken on the characteristics of a proxy war also makes it more difficult to find a peace solution for Ukraine. Just two months after the Russian invasion, for example, the US Secretary of Defense announced the goal of permanently weakening the Russian military forces.[127] From the US point of view, this goal is perhaps understandable, as it would cause lasting damage to another (former) great power – but it has nothing to do with solidarity or support for the Ukrainian population.

Rivalry between Russia and the US – or NATO – could also prevent steps towards sustainable peace in the future. At this point, we can't avoid looking at some of the bad decisions NATO has made over the past 30 years. I don't intend to downplay or justify the Russian war of aggression; I'd just like to pursue the question of what we could do better in the future.

Ever since the Soviet Union's collapse, Russia has ceased to be an equal partner to the West; at best it's been a third-rate counterpart. When it's come to both economic and security issues, the West has shown no interest in what Russia wanted or didn't want. One of the EU's most consequential decisions was rejecting the Russian proposal of creating a common economic area from Vladivostok to Lisbon in the early 2000s. That was at a time when Vladimir Putin was still allowed to speak in parliament and when he received a standing ovation there. And quite honestly, I have to say that as I'm writing that, I'm rereading it in disbelief, but that was what happened: Putin was cheered and applauded by all the parties in parliament, just two decades ago.

At the time, it was a conscious decision by the EU not to seek economic relations with Russia on an equal footing, but to enshrine an asymmetrical economic relationship, with Russia reduced to the status of a supplier of cheap oil and gas. From an economic point of view, this may have been logical. Russia was at rock bottom economically, and Germany in particular benefited immensely from the cheap fuel. But as I explained in Chapter 12, unjust economic relations are never a good basis for peaceful coexistence.

Russia's economic and security interests were never taken seriously after that. The Russian government felt threatened by the NATO missile defence system and NATO's expansion east. Whether we can understand and relate to this fear is irrelevant. As I described in Chapter 13 on disarmament and the Egon Bahr example, both sides' subjective security must be taken into account. During the Cold War, this worked well: in the course of the détente policy, steps were taken by both sides to avoid unwanted escalation. Since 1991, this hasn't been true in NATO's case.

The EU and NATO don't carry any blame for the current war of aggression in Ukraine, that's for sure. The decision for this attack, which violates international law, was made solely by the Kremlin, and it's the Kremlin that is responsible for it. But there is a responsibility in the EU and NATO to make decisions that will make a cooperative peace solution in Europe possible at some point in the future. And this won't happen if Russia continues to be treated as third-rate economically and in terms of security policy.

Then, and only then, will we have a chance of a more peaceful future in Europe, if we learn from the mistakes of the past 30 years and go back to the principles of détente: OSCE 2.0 rather than Cold War 2.0 – that's my vision for a peaceful Europe. The path to this goal is a very long one at the moment. First of all, it's vital to put down the weapons and achieve a just peace for the people of Ukraine.

15

PEACE NEEDS VISION: ISRAEL AND PALESTINE

I wrote part of this book in Jaffa, Tel Aviv, while I was working as a conflict analyst. On 7 October 2023 the sirens woke us at 6:33. Over the next few hours, horror stories about the Hamas massacre and the hostage-taking filtered through to us. Throughout the day there were repeated air raid warnings, and we saw explosions in the sky when the Iron Dome's defence missiles destroyed Hamas rockets. We had the luxury of being able to make our way overland to Jordan three days later, and fly to Germany from there.

Six months later, back in Jaffa, I was having a discussion with the Israeli filmmaker Yuval Abraham. He had made a film with his Palestinian colleague Basel Adra about the expulsion of Palestinians in the West Bank, for which they had just been awarded the prize for best documentary at the Berlinale. That evening, Yuval Abraham had to come alone because his colleague Basel Adra hadn't been given permission to enter Israel from his home in the West Bank: this was day-to-day discrimination under the occupation.

As we talked, Yuval Abraham summed up the great dilemma of all the current peace efforts in Israel: right now, most Israelis don't have the slightest notion of a peaceful solution. After the Oslo peace process in the 1990s, Israeli politics – and with it, society – has shifted further and further towards the right. The only answer people there see to the conflict with the Palestinians is in military strength and resilience. No party has dared to publicly support a peaceful, cooperative solution. Everyone was just looking to the next election results, so any criticism of the occupation, the settlements or the Gaza blockade would only have been detrimental. And, according to Abraham, that's taking its toll now: many people in Israel were deeply unsettled by the massacre. Contrary to expectations, the Israeli army's military strength and resilience wasn't able to protect them. At the same time, though, there are no ideas about any potential alternatives, because all thoughts of them have been completely banished from the prevailing politics over the last 20 years.

Yuval Abraham's analysis reminds me of what I said in the first chapter of this book: there needs to be an awareness that a peaceful way out is possible. Without a notion of a path down this route and of a common future, it is almost impossible to imagine a negotiated solution. It is precisely this notion that's lacking in the Israeli population at large – but it does exist, and it's a good notion. This is what this chapter's about: a vision of a peaceful future in Israel and Palestine.

I'm not a dreamer. I have no illusions at all about how difficult – for many even unimaginable – a lasting peace solution in the region is, especially in view of the sheer terror of 7 October, but also in view of Israel's current right-wing extremist government, where individual ministers are openly fulfilling their fantasies of a complete expulsion of all Palestinians.

On 7 October, there was dancing in the streets of Gaza and the West Bank, and when Iran attacked Israel with around 300 drones and missiles on 14 April 2024, shouts of 'Allahu Akbar' ('God is great') resounded in Palestinian Ramallah. As for the other side, the number one hit in Israel in December 2023 was the hip-hop creation 'Charbu Darbu', which translates as 'Destroy them'.[128] In one country they're singing about the total annihilation of the enemy, while in the other they're dancing in celebration of the terror. These aren't good starting points for a peaceful solution.

Beneath the surface, there are large wounds and scars on both sides that date back to 1948 and the founding of the nation of Israel. The expulsion of the Palestinians, the declarations of war and attacks against Israel by Arab neighbours, the occupation of the West Bank and the Gaza Strip in violation of international law, the broken Oslo process promises, the marauding settlers in the West Bank, the rocket attacks by Hamas, the terror of 7 October, which brought back the trauma of old pogroms for many Jews worldwide, the 30,000 dead and more in Gaza: we must acknowledge all these injustices, but they mustn't be an argument for new injustices by either side. The day-to-day brutality of the occupation can never justify the horror of 7 October, and the Hamas terror can never justify the total destruction of Gaza and the tens of thousands of deaths.

I have, and always have had, great sympathy for the Palestinian cause, but anyone who sees the massacre of 7 October as an act of liberation or justified resistance has lost their moral compass. On that very day, 7 October, someone wrote on Twitter: 'Show me how you fight, and I'll tell you what kind of social system you want.' There's scarcely a better way of putting it: the acts of kidnapping children, raping and murdering civilians indiscriminately don't indicate a good social model, and these aren't liberating actions, anywhere or in any way.

The Israeli–German historian Moshe Zimmermann published a book in early 2024 that is well worth reading. *Niemals Frieden?* (*Never Peace?*) – the question mark hinting at a small glimmer of hope – traces the last 30 years' developments in Israel towards the catastrophic situation now, and it's essentially a story of two hostage-takings: the one by Hamas on 7 October, but also the one by the right-wing extremist settlers who have been holding Israeli society hostage for 30 years. His book culminates by proposing a 'slightly different' two-state solution, against all odds. Moshe Zimmermann isn't a dreamer either; he starkly outlines the problems and stumbling blocks in a peace process. But he also mercilessly explains why it can't and won't work at all without a peace process of this kind when he writes in the book's final paragraph: 'the alternative would be a green light for another 7 October, another Afghanistan, or another Hiroshima.'

The thought of another Hiroshima makes me blanch, and yet it's not a million miles away. Sometimes, sitting at the kitchen table in Tel Aviv, I too have caught myself wondering whether I can really be quite sure that this war won't escalate to a nuclear level. After all, a right-wing radical minister has already been urging the Israeli government to drop an atomic bomb on Gaza.

If horrific scenarios like this are the alternative, we have no choice: we *must* think about ways to find a peaceful solution to the conflict, we must make them plausible, and we on the outside must do everything in our power to make them possible – as difficult as that may seem at the moment. And we must also be aware of the dangers of talking about potential visions: the present situation, in all its horror, must not be forgotten. Jerusalem-based journalist Nathan Thrall warns against a 'solutionism' that only discusses solutions and ignores the present:[129] that would ultimately play into the hands of the people who benefit from the status quo and don't want to change anything. It's an important objection, but it shouldn't mean we can't talk about visions at all, because, as I said, without the notion, without the image of a more peaceful future, it won't be possible.

Two states, one homeland

But what could a peaceful prospect actually look like? At the forefront of every discussion there's always the two-state solution as the goal: a state of Israel and a state of Palestine existing side by side. This was already provided for in the UN's partition plan of 1947; it was the basis of the Oslo peace talks in 1993; and it's still the official line of the EU and the US. And yet everyone agrees that the two-state solution has actually died a death, because the settlement policy of the last 30 years has brought about facts that seem almost impossible to change. 'Ignoring this is tantamount to denial of global warming,' as the Israeli-German philosopher Omri Boehm succinctly put it recently. In his book, he refers to a two-state *illusion*.[130]

There are now 700,000 Israeli settlers living in the West Bank; they would all have to be resettled by force for a two-state solution to work. And if you're thinking of a few wooden huts when you think of a settlement, you're very wrong: these are entire cities with large new housing estates and comprehensive infrastructures, where people have been building a new existence, in some cases for decades. It's hard to imagine them being evacuated. Making the settlements part of Israeli territory is similarly impossible: then Palestine would only be left with a patchwork of scarcely connected scraps of land.

This is why Moshe Zimmermann writes about a 'slightly different' two-state solution in his book. What something like this could look like in concrete terms has been worked out in some detail by a group of Israeli and Palestinian activists over recent years. Under the name A Land for All,[131] they have presented a new development of the two-state solution, which in my view has the potential for a genuine breakthrough – if there were desire from both sides for a peace process.

The Palestinian director of A Land for All, Rula Hardal, once summed up the organisation's basic goal as follows: 'We need more than peace in order to change the reality to be more equal or to bring more justice for the Palestinians and the Israeli people. That's why I don't like the word "peace". Peace is okay, it's nice, but it's not enough in this case. We need to speak about recognition, reconciliation, and the reality that has been established between the Israelis and the Palestinians during the last maybe 100 years.'[132]

Her proposal 'Two States, One Homeland' is rooted in these considerations. The land between the River Jordan and the Mediterranean is a historical and geographical entity for A Land for All, where the two groups – Palestinians and Israelis – could live together, but in two sovereign states within the 1967 borders. Citizens of both countries could move freely in both states, which together would be a homeland for all. According to this principle, a settler could become a citizen of Israel but carry on living in their settler apartment on Palestinian soil. Both countries could determine their own immigration policies. Jerusalem would have a special status as the capital of both countries, with its own joint local administration. The issue of external security would be organised by both states in a joint security council, while internally a joint supreme court would ensure that the respective minorities' rights in both states are guaranteed. A compensation mechanism would be developed for seized or confiscated property, which could be agreed to by all parties. The basic principle should be that old injustices cannot be healed with new ones.

A Land for All's proposals only set out a framework. On some points, they remain deliberately vague to avoid imposing too many restrictions on a potential peace process. In their model, the joint structures are relatively weak and have to compete with strong national parliaments or governments. According to one criticism, this cannot work in the long run, as the big issues of security and the extreme economic disparity between Israel and Palestine remain unresolved, and for this a strong central government is essential. In his book, Omri Boehm speaks of a one-state solution, a federal binational republic that he calls the 'Republic of Haifa', which is very similar to the Land for All model in its specific details.

Regardless of whether it's a slightly different two-state solution or a republic with two nations as a federation or confederation, what this structure would look like can only be clarified in an actual peace process. Only in serious negotiations will it become clear where the two sides' genuine, deep-seated needs lie and what could make a compromise solution possible.

Taking the red lines seriously

This proposal may sound utopian, but it does have a full range of advantages over the classic two-state solution. Above all, it replaces the previous narrative of separating the two nations with the paradigm of a common homeland with equal rights for all. It's an approach that may be more distant than ever for the vast majority of people in Palestine and Israel today, after almost eighty years of antagonism and fighting for their own separate states. But there can only be a genuine chance of lasting peace if the concept of antagonism is replaced by an understanding of common history and future.

A Land for All takes the realities on the ground very seriously. The settlers' interests, the division of Jerusalem and the economic imbalance between Israel and Palestine are taken into account. More than anything else, the proposal recognises the various red lines, in other words both sides' indispensable needs. On the Palestinian side, this means a state of their own, an end to the occupation, the displaced population's right to return, and compensation for the injustice they have suffered. On the Israeli side, this means the unrestricted right of all Jews worldwide to live in the Holy Land, the claim to the entire land of Israel, and security from any internal or external attacks.

Designating the entire area from the River Jordan to the Mediterranean as a common homeland for all Jews and Palestinians is more than simply intellectual sleight of hand. On the contrary – it's an irrefutable reality: for both groups, the entire country is the point of reference, expressed in the phrase 'From the river to the sea' for Palestinians, and for Israelis in the term 'Eretz Israel', the land of Israel.

Moshe Zimmermann explains in his book that Eretz Israel refers to the land and shouldn't be confused with the state of Israel. During the British Mandate, Zimmermann says, the full designation 'Palestine/Eretz Israel' was always used, in order to remain neutral. Both terms refer to all the land between the River Jordan and the Mediterranean Sea.

Any historical or archaeological attempt to grant one side or the other greater rights to this stretch of land by digging for relics is doomed to failure, although, absurdly, attempts are still being made to this day. Walking through the old city of Jerusalem, you can see how some houses are sinking as a result of archaeological excavations taking place in underground tunnels in search of definitive proof that Jews were there first. What a homeland is, though, is determined by head and heart, not centuries-old dust.

In contrast to the classic two-state solution, the proposal by A Land for All takes this intellectual and emotional claim to the entire country into account. Everyone would be able to move freely or settle on every square millimetre of Palestine/Eretz Israel if they wanted to, as citizens of one state or the other, but with equal rights and security. Full freedom of movement or settlement with protection of minorities and a jointly run court to monitor it: this is a more comprehensive and far-reaching solution than erecting a border fence that marks the proximity or confrontation of two states, each of which only covers part of the homeland it's claiming.

In danger and deep distress, the middle way spells certain death

A Land for All has the potential to revive the moribund two-state solution because the idea is firmly grounded in the realities in Palestine/Eretz Israel and it takes the indispensable needs of both sides into account. One of the masterminds and co-founders of this concept is Meron Rapoport, an Israeli journalist. He emphasises that their idea isn't a far-fetched dream; it's much closer to reality than all the other ideas that shape the Middle East debate. Basically, according to Rapoport, A Land for All has adopted the Schengen idea: different nationalities in a common space with freedom of movement and (almost) equal rights for all.[133]

The big question, of course, is what chances an idea like this might have, given the conflict's current escalation. Rula Hardal is certain that there's still support for a solution of this kind: 'Both people are tired from the death and from this violence and from the repeated waves of escalation. The two groups are tired from suffering, and especially the Palestinian people. They are the most to suffer in this situation, and they are the most interested in any solution more than the Israelis.'[134] Meron Rapoport is also certain that a majority would be in favour of this idea in Palestine today.

The situation in Israel is much more difficult. Rapoport says he has promoted the idea at hundreds of events over recent years. There was a great deal of approval, but the same questions almost always cropped up: Why? What's the point? That's irrelevant at the moment; peace isn't on the agenda. To get the discussion moving, Rapoport argues, a sense of urgency is needed, and this urgency has been absent from the vast majority of Israelis' consciousness for the past 25 years.

But then 7 October happened, and the deep shock sent through the Israeli population by the Hamas massacre could revive a search for solutions. Moshe Zimmermann writes in his book, '7 October 2023 proved it: if no negotiations take place, the opponents are in the waiting room to hell, in a manner of speaking.' And about Israel's relationship with its Arab neighbours, he says: 'Now, after the attack of 7 October, it is clear that sweeping the Palestinian issue under the carpet and wanting everything to be business as usual is not a solution.'

It's noticeable when Meron Rapoport talks that it almost physically pains him to view 7 October as a potential catalyst for reviving the two-state solution. But the fact is, he says, that this war, international pressure, and proceedings before the International Court of Justice have all created a new sense of urgency to find a different solution in Israel. Of course, calls for revenge and a consensus for the complete destruction of Gaza would still exist, whatever happens. But beneath the surface, Rapoport says, he can detect a deep sense of insecurity in almost every conversation. Where will this lead us? Will we survive this? He believes that this could lead to a change of heart: we've tried the status quo, we've tried military strength, we've tried the total destruction of Gaza – if none of this works, don't we need something new?

Time for optimism?

I have to admit that a deep pessimism about Palestine/Eretz Israel's future had a firm grip on me when I started writing this chapter. I was ready to write about a utopia, but only as a positive image far from any reality. The emotions on the ground are too strong on both sides, the warfare's too brutal and the mood is too charged. Objectively, practically none of the prerequisites for starting peace negotiations are in place, either. The conflict certainly isn't 'ripe', as Israel still firmly believes in victory, in the complete destruction of Hamas and in its own military strength. There's also a complete lack of trust, both between governments and between populations. There's no pressure from outside, and there's no concept of a potential alternative solution.

Genuine, living seeds of hope do exist, though. The village of Neve Shalom/Wahat al-Salam (Oasis of Peace) was founded back in the 1970s. Jewish and Palestinian families live there together, not only for historical reasons, but because together they want to show that they can, and that in spite of conflicts and difficulties, it's possible to be living proof of 'compassion, tolerance, and peace', as the Palestinian peace activist Rayek Ritzek writes in his book on the Oasis of Peace.[135] He, too, considers the Land for All proposal to be the most humane idea that's been put forward so far as a solution to the Israeli–Palestinian conflict.

But is it possible to make the leap from one small village to the whole country? Meron Rapoport insists that A Land for All is not a far-fetched utopia, but a genuine possibility. No matter how bleak the current situation may be, history sometimes takes sudden and radical turns. Rapoport explains how he started a new job as a journalist in early 1989, when Berlin was divided by a wall and Nelson Mandela was in prison in South Africa. A year later, the world was a different place: the Wall had fallen and Mandela was a free man. Again and again, Meron Rapoport comes back to the subject of Europe, and how arch enemies there were ultimately able to become partners and allies after centuries of war.

To ensure all this doesn't just remain mere words of encouragement, it's essential to actively do something to work towards a peace solution. A Land for All has set the ball rolling and put the idea of an escape route, the possibility of a solution, back on the agenda. Now it's crucial for us on the outside to instil these ideas deeper into the hearts and minds of the people in Israel and Palestine, and we need initiatives for new peace conferences and gentle pressure from donors on both sides so they can be open to a discussion process of this kind. None of this will happen quickly and the obstacles are great, but if we don't start today, we'll only have pessimism to offer tomorrow.

A Land for All, Moshe Zimmerman's 'slightly different' two-state solution and Omri Boehm's Republic of Haifa are all attempts to make a peaceful solution conceivable again – nothing more, nothing less.

Epilogue: Dispelling tanks from our thoughts

Peace is not just a dream. I didn't make up all the examples in this book. They are proof that many peaceful tools exist for resolving conflicts. Hardly any of them lead to success immediately, and even with them, it's still possible to fail – no question about it. But peaceful conflict resolution strategies do exist. Many of them have been tried in the past, and they can help prevent suffering, destruction and death in the future.

But far too rarely are they given a chance, because military thinking has become so dominant. For people who have nothing but tanks in their thoughts, every problem looks like a military one. As I said earlier, to a man with a hammer, every problem looks like a nail. How many times in the parliamentary Foreign Affairs Committee, when we were discussing a conflict situation somewhere in the world, did I have to sit through meetings where no one even asked how we could help resolve the conflict, asking instead whether we should send weapons, soldiers or both? This perspective is so narrow that the idea of a civil solution is no longer conceivable.

I'm certain – and writing this book has strengthened my conviction – that we could do plenty of things to make the world a little more peaceful. It would be enormously helpful if we stopped fuelling conflicts elsewhere in the world with unfair trade relations, detrimental manufacturing conditions or arms exports. That would be a very significant initial step.

Epilogue: Dispelling tanks from our thoughts

I'd like to live in a country where it's all about prioritising a civil approach: always look for a peaceful, civil solution first and take your finger off the trigger while you're thinking; a country that's respected all over the world, not for sending weapons or soldiers abroad but for sending peace experts, reconstruction aid and fair trade agreements. A peaceful foreign policy could and should adopt all of this. None of it is easy, and some of it comes at a cost – maybe money, but more than anything, political capital that we have to be willing to invest in peaceful solutions.

I want to live in a country that can afford this investment in peace, that doesn't stand idly by in the face of war crimes and human rights violations, but uses its power and experience to resolve conflicts peacefully, a country that doesn't pursue foreign policy as a military power or by supplying arms, but that uses all the possibilities outlined here to improve the chances of initiating peace negotiations without the need for military intervention.

I want to live in a country that is a force for peace. Whether we like it or not, the UK and Germany are powerful economic heavyweights, and have major influence in the world. Using this influence wisely means using it peacefully, and no one needs to worry about isolating themselves internationally with a solo pacifist effort. Japan has long since refuted this: until the 2010s, the country didn't export any weapons or send soldiers on foreign missions. No one could seriously claim that Japan's been isolated worldwide as a result.

I want to live in a country where the Minister of Health makes hospitals fit for people rather than war, where the Minister of Education proposes lessons on peace rather than civil defence exercises in schools, where the Ministry for Economic Affairs, rather than protecting the arms industry's interests, monitors them to safeguard peace in the world.

Making peace ourselves

When all the signs are pointing to a storm, when the disarmament architecture is in ruins, when Russia poses a genuine threat and there's an even greater threat from a new arms race, it's time to think against the grain and talk about disarmament. The current dynamics of public discussion in Europe is frightening, and there's almost nothing but talk of weapons, armament, defence and war capabilities. Pacifism has become a dirty word in many places. And, to reiterate, I'm not a radical pacifist rejecting all use of weapons under all circumstances and everywhere. I'm happy to acknowledge that there was no option other than armed struggle against Nazi Germany, and that there can be other situations where violence can no longer be tackled by peaceful means. They may be very rare, but they do exist. However, these historical exceptions must in no way tempt us to see every conflict only in a narrow military context. The peaceful, civil path should always remain our first choice: prioritising dialogue.

If we talk about disarmament in Europe today, we often hear a counterargument that it's out of the question to cut spending on the military, because of its dilapidated state and because of Russia's rapidly increasing military budget. But a quick look at the numbers shows a much more comforting picture: NATO currently has ten times the military expenditure of Russia. Even with a NATO without the USA – as threatened by Donald Trump – and even if we adjust the figures to account for relative buying power, the military advantages remain with the West: the European NATO countries have military expenditure of €430 billion, compared to 300 billion in Russia.[136]

Ten per cent for all

There is an idea about global disarmament that's been around for many decades, but which hasn't yet received the attention it's due: if all the countries in the world reduced their military spending by the same percentage at the same time, the relative security for each individual country would remain exactly the same. It wouldn't be a case of 100 tanks

Epilogue: Dispelling tanks from our thoughts

against 100 other tanks, but 90 against 90. The balance of power wouldn't change, so this idea works even with the prevailing thinking on security, and should also be acceptable to conservatives.

The current threat from Russia wouldn't contradict this, as 'all' means 'all', without exception. Europe would no longer be able to say, 'But what about Russia?' because Russia would be making the same cuts. The US would no longer be able to point the finger at China, China would no longer be able to point the finger at India, India would no longer be able to point the finger at Pakistan, and so on. If everyone lowers their spending at the same time, everyone wins – and saves a lot of money in the process.

According to the Swedish peace research institute SIPRI, over US$2.44 trillion was spent on military equipment worldwide in 2023. Even a one-off ten per cent reduction would mean a lot more money in every country's coffers. And reduced once by ten per cent, it would have a knock-on effect in the next few years: the plan would be to stay at this lower rate, rather than hike it back up after a year. Every year, the dollars saved could be invested in worthwhile things for everyone, instead of deadly weapons. 'Ten per cent for all' has precisely this double meaning: all the countries would reduce their arms spending by ten per cent, and all the people would benefit from the money saved. It sounds utopian, but that was also what people said about the call for a ban on landmines 30 years ago – and in the end it came good.

Ten per cent for all: it may sound like a utopia, but it is realistic and feasible if enough people work together to get it off the ground. Disarmament from below has often been a success in the past. The great powers in this world were against the ban on landmines; their military leaders' interest in these evil weapons was too great. Ultimately, though, a consortium of several nations and many NGOs set this ban in motion and achieved fantastic results. Today, even the US largely adheres to this ban. We did it then – I don't see why we shouldn't do it again.

And this would answer the question of how everything proposed in this book should be paid for: the universities specialising in peace expertise, the disarmament observatory, the biological weapons inspectorate, and much more. It will cost a lot of money – there's no doubt about it. A UK that's a force for peace doesn't come for free, just as there's no such thing as a UK that's a cost-free military power. The military mission in Afghanistan from 2001 to 2021 alone guzzled £27.7 billion.[137] If we just had this amount, just this £27.7 billion from one foreign mission, available to spend on peace work over the next 20 years, that would be £1385 million a year: an impressive sum that could be used to fund plenty of peace universities, disarmament observatories or inspection training. Peace is much cheaper than war. We just need to start.

All the heroes and heroines in this book, the Lian Gogalis, the Matthew Meselsons and the Milcah Lalams, all the peace researchers and so many others, can all be a shining example to us, proving it doesn't always take the UN or the world's greatest powers to create peace. Sometimes people like you and me are enough to change the course of the world together.

Jaffa, Tel Aviv, 28 May 2024

Acknowledgements

Many of the ideas, experiences and thoughts in this book have their roots in dozens of conversations over the past few years and decades, sometimes just a quick comment at an event, a mumbled sentence from a travel companion or a finger pointing in one direction or another. There are so many people I want to thank – I don't even know where to start.

Maybe it's best to start at the beginning. The biggest thanks go to my wife, Ramona Lenz. For everything, but also because she had the idea for this book, she contributed a lot of thoughts and ultimately fine-tuned my writing. Without you, this book would not exist.

My agent, Nina Sillem, didn't give up on me when I was sceptical about whether I really had enough meaningful things to say to fill a book. In hindsight, I have to say you were right, Nina, I did. Thank you.

Then there are all the many women and men involved in peace research and active peace work; I've learned so much from them, especially over the last year. They took the time to share their knowledge with me and pass on some bright ideas along the way. They were, in approximate chronological order: Matthew Meselson, Corinna Hauswedell, Sabine Kurtenbach, Elisa Satjukow, Christiane Fröhlich, Claudia Pfeifer Cruz, Niyazi Kızılyürek, Gabriele Gauler, Hannah Kiel, Gerald Schneider, Dastan Jasim, Janine Walter, Yaak Pabst, Karin Gerster, Muriel Asseburg, Ivesa Lübben, Stefan Liebich, Nina Potarska, Lüba Zakharov, Andreas Schüller, Usche Merk, Anne Jung, Florian

Eblenkamp, Christine Schweitzer, Gregor Gysi, Christin Lüttich, Natascha Zupan, Philip Poppelreuter, Lian Gogali, Evelyn Bahn, Yuval Abrahams, Meron Rapoport, Chris Whitman and Gil Shohat. I'd like to thank them all very much, as I know it's not always easy to spare the time for my questions.

Some of these conversations originally took place for our podcast dis:arm, so I'd like to give a big thank you to Linda Peikert, with whom I've been making this podcast since April 2023 (its subtitle is The Rosa Luxemburg Foundation Peace Talks).

I'd especially like to mention three former colleagues: Maria Oshana, Thomas Bockshecker and Alexander Lurz. They proofread large sections of my manuscript and gave me valuable tips. More than anything else, though, many ideas and thoughts in this book came together while I was working with them, and the other colleagues in our team. We worked together in the German parliament for years and exchanged ideas on an almost daily basis. Without you, I would never have had all these thoughts, and I'd never have been able to write this book. Thank you for the great times we've shared, for your sharp moral compasses and for being so patient with me.

I'd like to thank Stephan Hebel for the fascinating conversation we had, and for the information on the chapter 'News makes war'. Anna-Mia, Finn, Benson, Skyman and Lotti also read sections of the manuscript and contributed some really good ideas. In particular, they made sure that the book can be understood by people who weren't protesting in the Hofgarten in Bonn. Thank you!

Ulrich Wank edited the book with a great deal of empathy, and it's a much better book as a result. I'd like to thank him very much for that, as well, of course, as Ullstein Verlag and my editor Silvie Horch. Then, for the English version, I'd also like to thank Jo Heinrich, Sarah Braybrooke, Leonie Lock and Jane Rogers, who made it possible for you to hold this book in your hands right now.

NOTES

Introduction

1. Sumbeiywo, Lazaro (2009) 'To Be a Negotiator: Strategy and Tactics', Mediation Support Project. ETH-Zürich and swisspeace Bern. https://www.files.ethz.ch/isn/114828/negotiator.pdf.
2. Fisas, Vicenç (ed.) (2015) *Yearbook of Peace Processes*. Barcelona: Icaria Editorial, p. 9. https://peaceresourcecollaborative.org/wp-content/uploads/2019/10/Yearbook-on-Peace-Processes-2015.pdf. Another study concludes that 68% of all international wars between 1800 and 1980 ended through negotiation. Bramble, Alexander et al. (2023) *Negotiating an End to the War in Ukraine: Ideas and Options to Prepare for and Design a Negotiation Process*, Report. Geneva: Inclusive Peace. https://www.inclusivepeace.org/wp-content/uploads/2023/08/UKR-negotiations-preparations-report-2023.pdf.

1 What does it take to start peace negotiations?

3. ZEIT (2012) 'Syriens Vize deutet Verhandlungen über Assad-Rücktritt an' ('Syria's Vice President hints at negotiations over Assad's resignation'), in German only. ZEIT-online, 21 August 2012. https://www.zeit.de/politik/ausland/2012-08/syrien-assad-ruecktrittsverhandlungen.
4. Borger, Julian and Inzaurralde, Bastien (2015) 'West "ignored Russian offer in 2012 to have Syria's Assad step aside"', *The Guardian*, 15 September 2015. https://www.theguardian.com/world/2015/sep/15/west-ignored-russian-offer-in-2012-to-have-syrias-assad-step-aside.
5. Sumbeiywo, Lazaro (2009) 'To Be a Negotiator: Strategy and Tactics', Mediation Support Project. ETH-Zürich and swisspeace Bern, https://www.files.ethz.ch/isn/114828/negotiator.pdf.

6. Zartman, William (2001) 'The timing of peace initiatives: Hurting stalemates and ripe moments', *Global Review of Ethnopolitics* 1:8. https://doi.org/10.1080/14718800108405087.
7. Ferretti, Matthew (1990) 'The Iran–Iraq War: United Nations resolution of armed conflict', *Villanova Law Review* 35:197. https://digitalcommons.law.villanova.edu/vlr/vol35/iss1/3.
8. Bildt, Carl (2021) 'Bosnia to war, to Dayton, and to its slow peace', European Council on Foreign Relations. https://ecfr.eu/publication/bosnia-to-war-to-dayton-and-to-its-slow-peace/
9. Kurtenbach, Sabine (2023) 'Friedensgespräche' ('Peace talks'), in German only, dis:arm podcast, episode 1. https://www.rosalux.de/disarm
10. Fisher, Ron (2001) 'Methods of Third-Party Intervention', in *Berghof Handbook for Conflict Transformation*, p. 21. https://core.ac.uk/download/pdf/71735677.pdf.
11. Ischinger, Wolfgang (2023) 'Raus aus der Schockstarre – ein möglicher Weg zum Frieden in der Ukraine' ('Roused from a state of shock – a potential path to peace in Ukraine'), in German only, *Tagesspiegel* 12 March 2023. https://www.tagesspiegel.de/internationales/raus-aus-der-schockstarre-ein-moglicher-weg-zum-frieden-in-der-ukraine-9471989.html

2 Peace negotiations

12. Saying at the United Nations.
13. Herbolzheimer, Kristian (2015) 'The peace process in Mindanao, the Philippines: Evolution and lessons learned', Norwegian Peacebuilding Resource Centre (NOREF) report, December 2015. https://rc-services-assets.s3.eu-west-1.amazonaws.com/s3fs-public/a6c4f7339db9c90cd15a63c85405404e.pdf.
14. Naraghi Anderlini, Sanam (2012) 'Peace Negotiations and Agreements'. https://www.inclusivesecurity.org/wp-content/uploads/2012/04/37_peace_negotiations.pdf
15. Arnault, Jean (2001) 'Good Agreement? Bad Agreement? An Implementation Perspective'. https://www.studocu.com/en-za/document/university-of-south-africa/international-law/good-agreement-bad-agreement-arnault/17787787
16. Colchester, Felix et al. (2019) 'Implementing Peace Agreements: Supporting the Transition from the Negotiation Table to Reality'.

Discussion Points of the Mediation Support Network (MSN) no. 10. https://css.ethz.ch/content/dam/ethz/special-interest/gess/cis/center-for-securities-studies/pdfs/MSN%20Discussion%20Points%20Nr.10.pdf

17. Stone, Laurel (2014) 'Women Transforming Conflict: A Quantitative Analysis of Female Peacemaking'. https://papers.ssrn.com/sol3/papers.cfm?abstract_id=2485242
18. Sumbeiywo, Lazaro (2009) 'To be a Negotiator: Strategy and Tactics'. Mediation Support Project, ETH-Zürich and swisspeace Bern. https://peacemaker.un.org/sites/peacemaker.un.org/files/ToBeaNegotiator_Sumbeiywo2009.pdf
19. Mason, Simona and Siegfried, Matthias (2013) 'Confidence Building Measures (CBMs) in Peace Processes'. In: *African Union: Managing Peace Processes. A handbook for AU practitioners*, African Union, S. 61. https://hdcentre.org/wp-content/uploads/2016/07/AU-Handbook-Volume-I-Process-related-questions-July-2013.pdf
20. Bildt, Carl (2021) 'Bosnia to war, to Dayton, and to its slow peace'. European Council on Foreign Relations. https://ecfr.eu/publication/bosnia-to-war-to-dayton-and-to-its-slow-peace/
21. IPPNW (2024) 'Waffenstillstand und Frieden für die Ukraine. Eine Sammlung bestehender Vorschläge und möglicher Schritte, den Krieg in der Ukraine durch Diplomatie statt durch Waffen zu beenden' ('Ceasefire and peace for Ukraine. A collection of existing proposals and potential steps to end the war in Ukraine through diplomacy instead of weapons'), in German only. 6th edn, February 2024. https://www.ippnw.de/commonFiles/pdfs/Frieden/Waffenstillstand_und_Frieden_Ukrainekonflikt.pdf
22. UN General Assembly (2012) Resolution 66/290. https://www.un.org/humansecurity/wp-content/uploads/2022/06/N1147622.pdf
23. Wulf, Herbert (2023) 'Alles auf Sieg' ('All set for victory'), in German only. IPG Journal, 13 March 2023. https://www.ipg-journal.de/rubriken/aussen-und-sicherheitspolitik/artikel/alles-auf-sieg-6570/
24. Kurtenbach, Sabine (2023) 'Friedensgespräche' ('Peace talks'), in German only, dis:arm podcast, episode 1. https://www.rosalux.de/disarm
25. Ibid.
26. Sticher, Valerie (2022) 'Healing stalemates: The role of ceasefires in ripening conflicts'. *Ethnopolitics* 21:149. https://www.tandfonline.com/doi/full/10.1080/17449057.2022.2004776

27. UNDPPA (2022) 'Guidance on Mediation of Ceasefires' p. 11. https://peacemaker.un.org/documents/guidance-mediation-ceasefires
28. Herbolzheimer, 'The peace process in Mindanao'
29. Hauswedell, Corinna (2004) Der nordirische Friedensprozess – ein Modell? ('The Northern Irish peace process – a model?'), in German only). *Wissenschaft und Frieden* Dossier 45. https://wissenschaft-und-frieden.de/dossier/der-nordirische-friedensprozess-ein-modell/
30. Ingraham, Jeson (1998) The Irish Peace Process. CAIN Archive. https://cain.ulster.ac.uk/events/peace/talks.htm
31. Pfaffenholz, Thania et al. (2023) 'Negotiating an End to the War in Ukraine: Ideas and Options to Prepare for and Design a Negotiation Process'. Report for Inclusive Peace, pp. 17–18. https://www.inclusivepeace.org/wp-content/uploads/2023/08/UKR-negotiations-preparations-report-2023.pdf

3 Closing the wounds: justice for the victims

32. This quote and other information about Institut Mosintuwu comes from a discussion with Lian Gogali conducted on 30 November 2023. More information is available in this article about Lian Gogali: https://greennetwork.asia/figure/lian-gogali-brings-back-harmony-in-poso-with-schools-of-peace/. Her life has also been made into a film, *The Peace Agency*, https://peaceagencyfilm.com/
33. Discussion with Natascha Zupan on 11 January 2024. For further reading, her 2016 article 'Vergangenheitsarbeit' ('Transitional justice'), in German only, published by the Federal Agency for Civic Education, is highly recommended. https://www.bpb.de/themen/kriege-konflikte/dossier-kriege-konflikte/54742/vergangenheitsarbeit/. The article by Martina Fischer (2016), 'Aufarbeitung und Aussöhnung als Globale Aufgaben' ('Coming to terms and reconciliation as global tasks'), in German only, is also highly recommended. Brot für die Welt website, https://www.brot-fuer-die-welt.de/blog/2016-aufarbeitung-und-aussoehnung-als-globale-aufgaben/
34. UN (2023) 'Guidance Note of the Secretary General on Transitional Justice: A Strategic Tool for People, Prevention and Peace'. 11 October 2023 https://www.ohchr.org/en/documents/tools-and-resources/guidance-note-secretary-general-transitional-justice-strategic-tool

35. All information on international jurisdiction comes from a discussion with Dr Andreas Schüller from ECCHR, conducted on 14 February 2024. Available in episode 13 of the dis:arm podcast, March 2024 (in German only). https://www.rosalux.de/disarm
36. Medico International (2024) 'Haltbare Vorwürfe' ('Sustained accusations'), in German only. Interview with Andreas Schüller from ECCHR, 26 January 2024. https://www.medico.de/blog/haltbare-vorwuerfe-19366
37. ECCHR (2022) 'First criminal trial worldwide on torture in Syria before a German court'. https://www.ecchr.eu/en/case/first-criminal-trial-worldwide-on-torture-in-syria-before-a-german-court/
38. Seibert, Thomas (2020) 'Erinnern und dokumentieren. Hintergrundbericht über die Arbeit von AHRDO' ('Remembering and documenting. Background report on the work of AHRDO'), in German only. https://www.medico.de/blog/erinnern-und-dokumentieren-17795
39. Afghanistan Memory Home. https://afghanistanmemoryhome.org/
40. Burgess, Patrick (2018) 'Twenty Lessons from Twenty Years of Transitional Justice in Asia'. Study for the Indonesian NGO Asia Justice and Rights (AJAR). https://preview.asia-ajar.org/wp-content/uploads/2019/01/Twenty-Lessons-from-Twenty-Years-of-Transitional-Justice-in-Asia.pdf
41. Republic of The Gambia (2022) 'Government White Paper on the Report of the Truth, Reconciliation and Reparations Commission'. https://www.justiceinfo.net/wp-content/uploads/Gambia_White-Paper-on-TRRC-Report.pdf
42. Dale, Penny (2022) 'Gambia under Yahya Jammeh: Witch hunts, PTSD and veiled faces'. BBC, 12 June 2022. https://www.bbc.com/news/world-africa-61650362

4 Local conflict management

43. This chapter is based in part on a discussion with Dr Christine Schweitzer conducted on 16 November 2023. Much of this and more can be read in her excellent 2009 study 'Erfolgreich gewaltfrei' ('Successfully violence-free'), in German only, published by the Institut für Auslandsbeziehungen. https://www.ifa.de/fileadmin/Content/docs/mediathek/publikationen/erfolgreich-gewaltfrei.pdf

44. NIHCM (National Institute for Health Care Management Foundation) (2024) 'Gun Violence: The Impact on Society', infographic. https://nihcm.org/publications/gun-violence-the-impact-on-society. According to the report, there was a total of 42,967 firearm deaths in the US in 2023, of which 25,670 were suicides or accidents. Also John Gramlich (2023) 'What the data says about gun deaths in the U.S.', Pew Research Center. https://www.pewresearch.org/short-reads/2023/04/26/what-the-data-says-about-gun-deaths-in-the-u-s/
45. National Institute of Justice (2011) 'Program Profile: Cure Violence'. https://crimesolutions.ojp.gov/ratedprograms/205#summary
46. Nonviolent Peaceforce (2021) Civilians caught in crossfire: Your impact in the Philippines. https://nonviolentpeaceforce.org/civilians-caught-in-crossfire-your-impact-in-the-philippines/
47. Answer of the Federal Government of 12 December 2023 to the interpellation by the Member of the German Bundestag Cornelia Möhring (in German only). https://dserver.bundestag.de/btd/20/098/2009807.pdf, p.10.
48. Forum ZFD (2023) 'So kann es gehen – Deutschlands zivile Friedensfähigkeit stärken' ('Here's how it can work – building on Germany's civil peace capability'), in German only. https://www.forumzfd.de/de/zivileplanziele

5 UN peacekeeping forces: when trust hits rock bottom

49. Annan, Kofi (1999) 'Report of the Secretary-General pursuant to General Assembly Resolution 53/35: The Fall of Srebrenica'. Document number A/54/549 of 15 November 1999. Paragraph 503 https://www.securitycouncilreport.org/atf/cf/%7B65BFCF9B-6D27-4E9C-8CD3-CF6E4FF96FF9%7D/a_549_1999.pdf
50. Isler, Thomas (2018) 'Das historische Bild: Srebrenica, 12. Juli 1995' ('The historic picture: Srebrenica, 12 July 1995'), in German only. NZZ, 17 March 2018. https://www.nzz.ch/meinung/das-historische-bild-srebrenica-12-juli-1995-ld.1817486
51. UN Digital Library. https://digitallibrary.un.org/record/111999?v=pdf
52. UN profile of Dag Hammarskjöld, https://www.un.org/depts/dhl/dag/time1956.html

53. Melber, Henning (2015) 'Revisiting the "Hammarskjöld approach"'. *Development Dialogue* 2015/1:9. https://www.daghammarskjold.se/wp-content/uploads/2016/01/DHF_DD63_p9-15.pdf
54. United Nations: Background Iran-Iraq UNIIMOG. https://peacekeeping.un.org/mission/past/uniimogbackgr.html
55. Discussion with Niyazi Kızılyürek, 31 August 2023.
56. This section is based in part on discussions with Claudia Pfeifer Cruz from SIPRI on 20 July 2023 and 1 September 2023. Also available in episode 6 of the dis:arm podcast (in German only). https://www.rosalux.de/disarm
57. Boutros-Ghali, Boutros (1992) 'An Agenda for Peace: Preventive diplomacy, peacemaking and peace-keeping', UN Digital Library. https://digitallibrary.un.org/record/145749?v=pdf
58. *The Economist* (1996) 'The crossing of the Mogadishu line', 13 January. Also quoted in Charles Fowler (1999), 'The UN intervention in Somalia: Clausewitz crossing the Mogadishu line', National Defense University, Washington D.C. https://apps.dtic.mil/sti/pdfs/ADA432774.pdf
59. Meneo, Liz (2020) 'Forcing the UN to do right by Haitian cholera victims', *Harvard Gazette*, 6 October. https://news.harvard.edu/gazette/story/2020/10/a-decade-of-seeking-justice-for-haitian-cholera-victims/
60. Wheeler, Skye/Human Rights Watch (2020) 'UN peacekeeping has a sexual abuse problem', *The Hill*, 1 November. https://www.hrw.org/news/2020/01/11/un-peacekeeping-has-sexual-abuse-problem
61. UN (2023) 'A New Agenda for Peace. Our Common Agenda', Policy Brief 9. https://www.un.org/sites/un2.un.org/files/our-common-agenda-policy-brief-new-agenda-for-peace-en.pdf

6 Weapons inspections

62. This chapter is largely based on my work at UNMOVIC. Many details can be found in the extensive Compendium created and published by UNMOVIC when the work was over. The section on biological weapons can be found here: https://www.globalsecurity.org/wmd//library/news/iraq/un/unmovic-compendium_ch5.pdf
63. UN Document A/67/997 S/2013/553 of 16 September 2013. https://digitallibrary.un.org/record/756814?ln=en&v=pdf

64. UN (2023) 'Secretary General's Mechanism for Investigation of Alleged Use of Chemical and Biological Weapons (UNSGM)'. https://disarmament.unoda.org/wmd/secretary-general-mechanism/
65. Savary, Josef and van Aken, Jan (2022) 'Is Turkey violating the Chemical Weapons Convention?', report for IPPNW Germany, October. https://www.ippnw.de/commonFiles/bilder/Frieden/2022_IPPNW_Report_on_possible_Turkish_CWC_violations_in_Northern_Iraq.pdf

7 Using science against war propaganda

66. Davis, Tinsley (2004) 'Meselson and Stahl: The art of DNA replication', *Proceedings of the National Academy of Sciences* 101:17895
67. *New York Times* (1966) 'Scientists urge a weapons curb: 22 scientists bid Johnson bar chemical weapons in Vietnam', 20 September.
68. From Meselson's letter to President Johnson, autumn 1966. https://projects.iq.harvard.edu/files/meselsonarchive/files/1967_petition_to_johnson.pdf
69. The report by Meselson and his colleagues about their findings in Vietnam is available online here: https://www.nal.usda.gov/exhibits/speccoll/items/show/1953?advanced%5B0%5D%5Belement_id%5D=49&advanced%5B0%5D%5Btype%5D=is+exactly&advanced%5B0%5D%5Bterms%5D=legislation&sort_field=added&sort_dir=d
70. Quoted in Jonathan Tucker (2001) 'The 'Yellow Rain' controversy: Lessons for arms control compliance', *Nonproliferation Review*, Spring, S. 25–42. https://www.nonproliferation.org/wp-content/uploads/npr/81tucker.pdf
71. Guillemin, Jean (2001) *Anthrax: The Investigation of a Deadly Outbreak*. Berkeley, CA: University of California Press

8 News makes war

72. MacArthur, John (1992) 'Remember Nayirah, witness for Kuwait?', *New York Times*, 6 January 1992. https://www.nytimes.com/1992/01/06/opinion/remember-nayirah-witness-for-kuwait.html
73. WDR (1992) *Erster Irakkrieg: Die Baby-Lüge der USA* (*The First Iraq War: The USA's Baby Lie*), in German only. https://www1.

wdr.de/mediathek/video/sendungen/video-erster-irakkrieg-die-baby-luege-der-usa--102.html
74. IAEA (International Atomic Energy Agency) (2011) 'Implementation of the NPT Safeguards Agreement and relevant provisions of Security Council resolutions in the Islamic Republic of Iran', GOV/2011/65, 8 November. https://www.iaea.org/sites/default/files/gov2011-65.pdf
75. Pajdak, Karolina (2011) 'Können die Atom-Raketen der Mullahs auch uns treffen?' ('Can the mullahs' atomic weapons hit us too?'), in German only. *Bild* online, 9 November. https://www.bild.de/politik/ausland/atomprogramm-iran/iran-atombericht-raketen-reichweite-israel-europa-ahmadinedschad-droht-der-welt-20889654.bild.html
76. It literally states: 'We judge with high confidence that in fall 2003, Tehran halted its nuclear weapons program.' US National Intelligence Council (2007) 'National Intelligence Estimate – Iran: Nuclear Intentions and Capabilities'. https://www.dni.gov/files/documents/Newsroom/Reports%20and%20Pubs/20071203_release.pdf
77. Dilanian, Ken (2011) 'Iran has technical means to make nuclear bomb, IAEA says'. *Los Angeles Times*, 7 November. https://www.latimes.com/nation/la-xpm-2011-nov-07-la-fg-iran-nuclear-report-20111108-story.html
78. For example, *Der Spiegel*, 6 July 2018: 'OPCW weist Spuren von Chlorgas in Duma nach' ('OPCW detects traces of chlorine gas in Douma'), in German only. https://www.spiegel.de/politik/ausland/syrien-giftgasangriff-in-duma-opcw-weist-spuren-von-chlorgas-nach-a-1217175.html
79. OPCW (2018) 'Interim Report of the OPCW Fact-Finding Mission Syria Regarding the Incident of Alleged Use of Toxic Chemicals as a Weapon in Douma, Syrian Arab Republic, on 7 April 2018', S/1645/2018, published 6 July 2018. https://www.opcw.org/sites/default/files/documents/S_series/2018/en/s-1645-2018_e_.pdf
80. Hebel, Stephan (2021) 'Wahrhaftigkeit braucht Standpunkte' ('Truthfulness needs a point of view'), in German only. In Richard Meng, Thomas Kaspar (eds) (2021) *Haltung zählt*, edition 7, Berlin, pp. 89–97

9 Arms exports out of control

81. Details on the regulation of arms exports in the UK can be found in the paper 'An introduction to UK arms exports'. https://research-briefings.files.parliament.uk/documents/CBP-8312/CBP-8312.pdf
82. Hempel, Klaus (2021) 'Illegaler Waffenexport: Sig Sauer muss Millionenbetrag zahlen' ('Illegal weapons exports: Sig Sauer has to pay out millions'), in German only. *Tagesschau*, 1 July https://www.tagesschau.de/inland/sig-sauer-bundesgerichtshof-101.html
83. *Der Spiegel* (1978) 'Das ist doch wirklich schwarzer Humor' ('That is truly black humour', in German only). Interview with Franz-Josef Strauss, 16 July. https://www.spiegel.de/politik/das-ist-doch-wahrlich-schwarzer-humor-a-86a84bbc-0002-0001-0000-000040942726
84. https://www.bbc.co.uk/news/business-35834473
85. https://caat.org.uk/alternatives/jobs/
86. https://www.statista.com/statistics/520592/spirits-and-liqueurs-export-value-united-kingdom-uk/
87. https://oec.world/en/profile/country/gbr
88. https://www.adsgroup.org.uk/knowledge/value-of-aerospace-defence-security-and-space-sectors-to-uk-economy-increased-50-in-last-10-years-new-data-finds/
89. https://questions-statements.parliament.uk/written-questions/detail/2024-10-08/8024
90. https://caat.org.uk/alternatives/jobs/#:~:text=Arms%20industry%20jobs,a%20figure%20of%20300%2C000%20jobs.
91. https://www.common-wealth.org/interactive/lucas-plan-map
92. https://www.counterfire.org/article/made-in-britain-tory-profiteering-from-iran-iraq-war/
93. van Aken, Jan (2019) 'Der Heckler & Koch-Prozess: Eine Zusammenfassung' ('The Heckler & Koch Trial: A summary'), in German only. https://www.rosalux.de/publikation/id/39861/der-heckler-koch-prozess-eine-zusammenfassung
94. The figures are derived from the government's answers to several written interpellations from members of the Bundestag in September 2013, including interpellation 39 (p. 6) in Bundestag document 17/14777. https://dserver.bundestag.de/btd/17/147/1714777.pdf
95. https://www.bbc.co.uk/news/uk-28212724

96. Answer of the Federal Government to Written Interpellations Nos 80 and 81, October 2013.

11 Sanctions and their side effects

97. This chapter is based in part on a discussion with Professor Gerald Schneider on 2 October 2023, available in the dis:arm podcast, episode 7 (in German only). https://www.rosalux.de/disarm
98. UN Security Council Resolution 661 of 6 August 1990. https://digitallibrary.un.org/record/94221?v=pdf
99. Ali, Mohamed M. et al. (2003) 'Annual mortality rates and excess deaths of children under five in Iraq, 1991–98', *Population Studies* 57:217
100. Dastan Jasim in the dis:arm podcast, episode 7 (in German only). https://www.rosalux.de/disarm
101. Piketty, Thomas (2022) 'The western elite is preventing us from going after the assets of Russia's hyper-rich', *The Guardian*, 16 March. https://www.theguardian.com/commentisfree/2022/mar/16/russia-rich-wealthy-western-elites-thomas-piketty
102. Hufbauer, Gary et al. (2019) *Economic Sanctions Reconsidered*. Peterson Institute for International Economics.
103. van Aken, Jan (2022) 'Wie werken Sanktionen?' ('What do sanctions actually do?'), study for the Rosa Luxemburg Foundation, 23 September. https://www.rosalux.de/en/news/id/47016
104. Gehrcke, Wolfgang et al. (2017) 'Für eine neue Ostpolitik Deutschlands' ('For a New German Ostpolitik'), in German only. Motion from the parliamentary group Die Linke in the German Bundestag, document 18/11167. https://dserver.bundestag.de/btd/18/111/1811167.pdf
105. Wagner, Katharina (2022) 'Wladimir Potanin: Der Oligarch ohne Sanktionen' ('Vladimir Potanin: The oligarch without sanctions'), in German only, *Frankfurter Allgemeine Zeitung*, 31 May. https://www.faz.net/aktuell/wirtschaft/unternehmen/ukraine-krieg-wladimir-potanin-ist-der-oligarch-ohne-sanktionen-18071395.html
106. Kiel, Hannah (2023) 'Unilateral Sanctions in International Law', background study for the Rosa Luxemburg Foundation New York. https://rosalux.nyc/international-sanctions/

12 War starts here. Peace too

107. INKOTA (2022) 'Niedrige Kakaopreise und Einkommen für Kakaobäuer' ('Low cocoa prices and income for cocoa farmers'), in German only. https://makechocolatefair.org/probleme/niedrige-kakaopreise-und-einkommen-fuer-kakaobaeuerinnen
108. German Cocoa Trade Association (2020) 'Annual Report 2019/2020', p. 7, in German only. https://www.kakaoverein.de/files/kakaoverein/doc/Kakaoverein_Gesch%C3%A4ftsbericht_2019-2020_digital.pdf
109. Bundeszentrale für politische Bildung (BPB) and Bonn International Center for Conversion (BICC) (2012) 'Bitterer Kakao – Landwirtschaftliche Produkte als Konfliktrohstoffe' ('Bitter cocoa – Agricultural products as conflict minerals'), in German only. https://sicherheitspolitik.bpb.de/de/m4/articles/bitter-cocoa-agricultural-products-as-conflict
110. Johnson, Dominic (2006) 'Aufrüstung dank Kakao' ('Armament through cocoa'), in German only, *Die Tageszeitung*, 20 January, p. 3. https://taz.de/!486656/
111. Scherrer, Christoph (2022) 'Krieg als Folge des Konkurrenprinzips?' ('War as a consequence of the competitor principle?'), in German only, *Makronom – Online-Magazin für Wirtschaftspolitik*. https://makronom.de/geooekonomie-krieg-als-folge-des-konkurrenzprinzips-42723
112. Heidelberg Institute for International Conflict Research (2023) 'Conflict Barometer 2022'. https://hiik.de/conflict-barometer/current-version/?lang=en
113. Jung, Anne (1999) 'Angola: die Anatomie eines Mega-Verbrechens' ('Angola: the anatomy of a mega-crime'), in German only. https://www.medico.de/angola-die-anatomie-eines-mega-verbrechens-13935
114. Jung, Anne (2004) 'Die glänzenden Seiten des Krieges – Rohstoffausbeutung in Afrika' ('The shining sides of war – exploitation of raw material in Africa'), in German only, in 'Afrika: Lizenz zum Plündern. Materialien für eine Veranstaltung am Grips-Theater', p. 10. http://www.gegenstimmen.de/20040616/Afrika_15.06.04.pdf
115. Bundesanstalt für Geowissenschaften und Rohstoffe (BGR) (2009) 'Coltan: Herkunftsnachweis von Columbit-Tantaliterzen'

('Coltan: Proof of origin of columbite tantalite ores'), in German only. https://www.geozentrum-hannover.de/DE/Themen/Min_rohstoffe/Projekte/Lagerstaettenforschung-abgeschlossen/LF_Herkunftsnachweis_COLTAN.html

116. Weimerskirch, Henri et al. (2020) 'Ocean sentinel albatrosses locate illegal vessels and provide the first estimate of the extent of undeclared fishing', *Proceedings of the National Academy of Sciences* 117:3006. https://www.pnas.org/doi/full/10.1073/pnas.1915499117

117. Vinciguerra, Venusia (2011) 'How the Daewoo Attempted Land Acquisition Contributed to Madagascar's Political Crisis in 2009', paper presented at the International Conference on Global Land Grabbing at the University of Sussex. https://www.future-agricultures.org/wp-content/uploads/pdf-archive/Venusia%20Vinciguerra.pdf

118. Ziegler, Jean (2005) *Das Imperium der Schande* (*The Empire of Shame*), in German only. Munich: Bertelsmann Verlag.

13 Disarmament from above and from below

119. Bundeszentrale für Politische Bildung (BPB) (2019) 'Vor 40 Jahren: Der SALT-II-Vertrag zur Rüstungsbegrenzung' ('40 years ago: the SALT II Arms Limitations Treaty'), in German only. https://www.bpb.de/kurz-knapp/hintergrund-aktuell/292612/vor-40-jahren-salt-ii-vertrag-zur-ruestungsbegrenzung/

120. Atmann, Jürgen et al. (2001) 'Präventive Rüstungskontrolle' ('Preventive Arms Control'), in German only, Wissenschaft & Frieden, Dossier No. 38. https://wissenschaft-und-frieden.de/dossier/praeventive-ruestungskontrolle/

121. Discussion with Anne Jung, Medico International, on 14 November 2023, parts of which are available in the dis:arm podcast, episode 14 (in German only). https://www.rosalux.de/disarm

122. Ihl, Cornelia and van Aken, Jan (2024) 'Droht ein neues Wettrüsten?' ('Is there a threat of a new arms race?', short study by the Rosa Luxemburg Foundation on rearmament, in German only. https://www.rosalux.de/publikation/id/51913/droht-ein-neues-wettruesten.

14 Peace for Ukraine?

123. Zelik, Raul (2023) 'Die Linkspartei wird derzeit in der Ukraine-Debatte leider kaum wahrgenommen' ('Unfortunately the Left Party is scarcely noticed in the Ukraine debate right now'), in German only, *Der Freitag*, 1 February. https://www.freitag.de/autoren/raul-zelik/die-linkspartei-wird-derzeit-in-der-ukraine-debatte-leider-kaum-wahrgenommen
124. Demirjian, Karoun (2022) 'Milley tries to clarify his case for a negotiated end to the Ukraine war', *Washington Post*, 16 November. https://www.washingtonpost.com/national-security/2022/11/16/milley-ukraine-negotiate/
125. Discussion with Mike Milley at the Economic Club of New York, 683rd Meeting, 9 November 2022.
126. Fuhrmann, Johann and Herold, Heiko (2022) 'China's Dilemma' ('China's dilemma'), in German only, Konrad Adenauer Foundation Beijing. https://www.kas.de/de/web/china/laenderberichte/detail/-/content/chinas-dilemma
127. Ryan, M. and Timsit, A. (2022) 'U.S. want Russian military "weakened" from Ukraine invasion, Austin says', *Washington Post*, 25 April. https://www.washingtonpost.com/world/2022/04/25/russia-weakened-lloyd-austin-ukraine-visit/

15 Peace needs vision: Israel and Palestine

128. Kessler, Dana (2024) Life During Wartime. Tablet, 4 January 2024. https://www.tabletmag.com/sections/community/articles/life-during-wartime-tel-aviv
129. Nathan Thrall, at an event hosted by medico international, 7 May 2024. https://twitter.com/i/spaces/1DXxyjNpOrvKM
130. Boehm, Omri (2020) *Israel – eine Utopie* (*Israel – A Utopia*), in German only. Berlin: Propyläen Verlag.
131. https://www.alandforall.org
132. Hardal, Rula (2023) 'Life as a Palestinian Citizen of Israel', interview with the Center for Strategic and International Studies, 28 November. https://www.csis.org/analysis/rula-hardal-life-palestinian-citizen-israel
133. Discussion with Meron Rapoport on 28 April 2024.
134. Hardal, op. cit.

135. Ritzek, Rayek R. (2017) *The Anteater and the Jaguar*, Createspace Independent Publishing Platform.

Epilogue: Dispelling tanks from our thoughts

136. https://www.yahoo.com/news/greenpeace-study-says-nato-still-075729855.html?guccounter=1&guce_referrer=aHR0cHM6Ly93d3cuZ29vZ2xlLmNvbS8&guce_referrer_sig=AQAAAGwq1Hpl3e7_XIP1J2FEHCEIPCYGm2muYKbPTS25_kNvFPjjKvMIS-BPJS-KA59U1bcILg_ixTcpE7RLzlJmkL263vcZcAVnUgdINI3Nj-3j__nlAePjPJ7DyFWV_JHo6GhZfzSYj5BNSdyvSEAPu25BQFI9xJ1Kr7Q3L53jazPLB
137. https://commonslibrary.parliament.uk/research-briefings/cbp-9298/

AUTHOR BIO

© Julien Then

Jan van Aken, who holds a PhD in biology, worked as a genetic engineering expert for Greenpeace and as a biological weapons inspector for the United Nations from 2004 to 2006. From 2009 to 2017, he was a member of parliament in Germany for the Left Party. He then worked as a policy advisor in International Conflict Analysis at the Rosa Luxemburg Foundation in the Middle East. Since October 2024, he has served as co-chairman of the Left Party.

Jo Heinrich lives near Bristol with her family and translates from German and French. Her translations include Katja Oskamp's *Marzahn, Mon Amour*, which won the 2023 Dublin Literary Award and was shortlisted for the Warwick Prize for Women in Translation. She has also translated Oskamp's *Half Swimmer* and *The Invention of Good and Evil* by Hanno Sauer, and she was part of a team translating Angela Merkel's memoirs, *Freedom*.